THAT SUCKS...
WHAT NOW?

REAL-WORLD SOLUTIONS FOR GETTING
THROUGH WHAT YOU'RE GOING THROUGH

SCOTT SCHILLING
FOREWORD BY JACK CANFIELD

THAT SUCKS... WHAT NOW?

Quantity sales special discounts are available on quantity purchases by corporations, associations, and others. For details, contact the publisher at the address above.

Orders by U.S. trade bookstores and wholesalers. Email info@ BeyondPublishing.net

The Beyond Publishing Speakers Bureau can bring authors to your live event. For more information or to book an event contact the Beyond Publishing Speakers Bureau speak@BeyondPublishing.net

The Author can be reached directly BeyondPublishing.net/ AuthorScottSchilling

Manufactured and printed in the United States of America distributed globally by BeyondPublishing.net

BEYOND

New York | Los Angeles | London | Sydney

ISBN Dust Jacket: 978-1-949873-42-9

ISBN Softcover: 978-1-949873-75-7

Praise for
THAT SUCKS...WHAT NOW?

"That Sucks—What Now? is an all-encompassing read filled with loving wisdom, and heartfelt sharing from the author.

I was utterly amazed at how much information is shared in such a practical way! If you're facing a challenge of any kind, this book will guide you through that darkness. An uplifting must read!"

Robert Clancy
International Best-Selling Author of The Messenger,
and Co-host of The Mindset Reset Show

"Scott has been through unreasonable challenges and always chooses to be an overcomer! He looks for the opportunity in the obstacle and the blessing in the disappointment.

He's been faithful despite his circumstances, counting it joy even when his situation did not look good! You will be encouraged no matter where you are in life."

Kelli Calabrese
Best-Selling Author of Mom and Dadpreneurs, Wellness Mompreneur

"Read this book! Scott gives you inspiring stories that will help you deal with the challenges of life and a simple road map to get through them. A must read!"

Dr. Fabrizio Mancini
International Best-Selling Author, Speaker and Media Personality

"Reading this book helped me realize that if someone as incredible as Scott can have these challenges and be as brilliant as he is, then I too can create massive results! Thank you, Scott, for sharing the reality of life, and encouraging us to do more with our own."

Tonya Hofmann
CEO & Co-Founder of BeeKonnected.com

"Scott Schilling delivers the gold again! In this upbeat no nonsense guide to persisting through life's stuff while living from a grateful heart and positive mind, he shows by experience that those who persevere do so on purpose.

A great read for the conscious leader who's ready to find the true power and meaning of B.A.L.A.N.C.E for their life and business."

Lia Dunlap
The Oracle on Purpose

"Scott Schilling is a competent and highly successful businessman who I was blessed to meet at a conference in Las Vegas years ago. He is a gifted teacher who has lived a fascinating life and has faced and conquered seemingly insurmountable challenges.

In this book, Scott shares intimately from his own experiences how to best process problems and live our best lives. Get yours today!"

Eddie Smith
Owner & CEO, Worldwide Publishing Group, LLC

"One of the greatest collections of lifelong wisdom I've ever seen...just amazing!"

Dr. Greg Reid
Author: Think and Grow Rich Series

"JP & Associates Realtors® was born around a simple concept, supply real estate agents everything they could possible want or need in a brokerage. Scott, his books and trainings are much the same.

He uses his personal experiences good, bad or ugly to pass along the solutions learned for the good of his students. As the title implies, this book is full of real-world solutions to real-world challenges."

JP Piccinini
CEO & Founder JP & Associates Realtors®

"I've known Scott for years. From the first time we met, we hit it off because we share a servant's heart. I founded BeSomeone.org to help inner city youth learn to use Chess as a metaphor for life and utilize Brains Over Bullets.

When learning what we were doing, Scott immediately helped by including Be Someone in his book, "*Talking with Giants!*" raising both awareness and money for the cause. If you can learn from Scott, as they say, "Just Do It!"

Orrin C. Hudson
Executive Director, Be Someone, Inc.

"If you want to become the kind of person who can consistently overcome life's toughest challenges and win the mental battles that keep you feeling stuck & confused, READ THIS BOOK!

No matter what you've been through or what you're going through, you're just one thought away from transforming your life forever."

Brian Fleming
Combat-Wounded Afghanistan War Veteran - Suicide Bombing Survivor - Author & International Speaker

"There's a myth that experience is the great teacher. The truth is EVALUATED experience is the great teacher. The expensive way to learn is to make a mistake. The inexpensive way to learn is from other people's mistakes. *That Sucks - What Now?* will add value!"

Logan Stout
Entrepreneur, Best-Selling Author, Speaker, Influencer, Mentor

"A MUST READ Powerful, Inspirational, Overcoming Personal Life Change, Heartfelt, Equal Real Circle of Life for Everyone Today.

Scott Schilling's personal solutions will definitely impact you and the world for generations to come, you will feel Scott's energy resonating through every page. Scott's Real Experience Journey will relate to every soul on the planet.

Thank you for this wonderful opportunity for helping mankind with your Real-World Solution Tools."

Marc Cohen
Chairman / Founder/ CEO / Buy Direct Companies: Global Visionary Influencer, Strategic Intelligence Advisor

"*That Sucks What Now?* came from the heart as a result of Scott living through some unimaginable challenges. His willingness to share his stories publicly is valuable in so many ways.

Scott lays out the secrets, the success techniques, the strategies and the tips on how to live and thrive through the challenges that come our way.

Claiming victory in the good times is easy. Creating victory in the middle of adversity is hard. The mental toughness, the mindset, the persistence and the dedication required is what you'll learn from Scott's experience."

Mark Johnson
Chief Executive Officer - JP and Associates REALTORS®

"Scott Schilling knows as well as anyone that life can change in an instant. His personal physical experience brought him to a very low point in his life. What happened is that Scott learned quickly how to deal with life when it throws you its worst, how to cope, recover, and move through it.

Scott provided some excellent wisdom on how to make life amazing every day no matter what comes our way. A must read for those going through challenging times."

Rich Cavaness
Author of The Gratitude Effect and Power to Thrive

"A must read for every entrepreneur. *That Sucks... What Now?* is a bridge Scott has built to make our lives more manageable and easier to navigate.

A personal guide for overcoming obstacles in business and life. Scott has used experiences to help everyone move from guessing to knowing, a must for success in all we do."

Richard Eckermann
Co-Owner, Co-Founder, VP of Sales & Marketing - Focus on the 5

"Scott Schilling shares from a place of authenticity and wisdom along with a proving roadmap for all those wanting to navigate the entrepreneur's journey. Resilience, persistence, faith and action are all part of the necessary tools you will need. Thank you, Scott, for sharing your roadmap and wisdom!

Kyle Wilson
Strategist, Best-Selling Author,
Founder of Jim Rohn International & KyleWilson.com

"*That Sucks - What Now?* is brilliant, practical, and deeply insightful. A must-read guidebook for the contribution-conscious leader who is ready to get out of their own way and use their divine experiences to pay it forward in profound ways that change the world.

When you absorb the profound wisdom and real-life tools for powerful living and leading, you'll never be the same."

Lisa Mininni
Best-Selling Author & President,
Excellerate Associates & Founder, The Business Innovation Lab

"What a beautiful, vulnerable and powerful book! I've known Scott for years and watched him consistently take on and push through various challenges in both life and business. It's inspiring to watch Scott lean into the challenges, and also master the lessons learned coming through them.

His heart is dedicated to sharing those real-world solutions to benefit others. This book captures that real-life knowledge and shares in such a way that anyone can implement it in their lives...impressive! And destine to become a classic!"

Teresa de Grosbois
International Best-Selling Author of Mass Influence.

"There is no doubt when the "S**t hits the fan" in your life you want all the wisdom and maturity surrounding you possible. When our company "Focus on the 5" set out to find "THE COACH" advisor for the Face and Voice of 5%ers, Scott was the name and leader that we came up with. People like Scott are who you want at your side.

If you ever get a chance to meet him, first thing you will feel is a genuineness and sincerity to help you and others, mankind in general. He is Immersed in Faith of God. Scott is born to be a spiritual wisdom Coach, Leader of Giants, Risk Takers, Entrepreneurs, Leaders, Visionaries, Driven Souls.

I believe this Book came from a place in him that will make an impact on the world.

Ken Coleman
Founder – Focus on the 5

There are quite a few moments in Scott's book that I truly felt well, "*That Sucks - What Now?*" Then in the next instant I was inspired by Scott's humble real-life acceptance and desire to just pick himself up and continue on with his life's journey.

The book is filled with lessons of faith, determination and wisdom, the type of wisdom of only those few brave souls that have stumbled many, many times in their lifetime and still manage to pick themselves up and carry on with life's possibilities!

L. Neil Thrussell
International Best-Selling Author - A Warrior's Heart

DEDICATION

"That Sucks...What Now?" is dedicated to so many who have been true inspirations in my life. Their "servant hearts" are a model of what we should all emulate.

First, to my lovely and beautiful wife, Peggy, who has been my rock through all my endeavors. Peggy has supported me no matter what the task or challenge. Her love and support have kept me going, especially in times of difficulty. We've also had so many amazing times together enjoying this gift called life.

To my father, Bill, mom Mary-Jane, brother Bruce, who invested in me for years across all areas of life and business. To my sister, Marilyn, who has worked to invest in people to help give them a better path. Her input in crafting this material was invaluable.

To my daughter, Jordan, for her spirit, laughter and "want to" when it comes to anything she decides to accomplish. Jordan is an inspiration because of her desire to help bring up those around her when they need it. She only gets better as she experiences more.

To my son, Taylor, for his amazing heart, light and desire to help others. He is an inspiration with all he has accomplished at such a young age.

To Jack Canfield for his love, support, guidance and friendship in helping me grow and understand that we all have unlimited potential. That we can accomplish anything we focus our minds on and take action to achieve.

And finally, to so many more that it is impossible to list all by name...you know who you are! It is with deep gratitude and love that this book is dedicated to those above, and to all people these works might come to touch.

Thank you all for bringing so much into my life and the lives of so many others!

TABLE OF CONTENTS

Foreword By
JACK CANFIELD

Hi! Jack Canfield here. You probably know me as the cofounder of the *Chicken Soup for the Soul®* book series that has sold more than 500 million copies since its inception in 1993. What you may not know is that over the years, thousands of people have come through my training programs and been exposed to my work through my bestselling books like *The Success Principles™*, *The Power of Focus*, and *The Aladdin Factor*.

I've had a passion for helping people achieve their goals and live their highest vision for many years. And rarely have I seen an individual absorb, formulate and execute the principles and strategies I've taught to the level that Scott Schilling has.

Scott has taken much of the information and many of the techniques he has learned from me and his many other mentors, and put them into action in his own life. He fully lives every one of the things he speaks, trains and writes about. He also has a deep desire and commitment to share his experiences with all those who want to learn.

As a longtime member of my Platinum Inner Circle and student community, Scott has always shown his willingness and enthusiasm to learn everything he can and grow as much as he could. He eagerly seeks out information, evaluates it and implements it in his life. He is truly committed to the principle of constant and never-ending personal improvement in his life and his work. And more importantly, he always wants to teach what he has learned to help create a better world for everyone.

Some 16 years ago, while Scott was still in corporate America, I had the pleasure of sharing the same speaking platform with him as he was launching his speaking career. What I witnessed was a level of drive and talent in him that I had seldom seen in others. It became very apparent to me that he had far greater capacity to make a difference than he was able to accomplish in his position in the corporate world. As his new mentor, I made the decision to call Scott on it and challenge him to do more. I suggested that he was not fulfilling everything he was put here on the earth to do, and that to a certain extent, he was just coasting as long as he stayed in his corporate job. He was living a nice life, but he wasn't using all the talents and capabilities that God had granted him. He had so much more to give.

We actually had the "money talk" he refers to in this book. This is where I shared that everyone has the obligation to make as much money as they possibly can, not for the sake of the money, but for the two things that come with it—the influence that comes along with having money so you can create more positive impact where it's needed and the good things that you can do with that money for the others you care about. Obviously when you have more money than you need, the excess can be contributed back to those who don't have the opportunity or ability to generate it themselves. Used properly, money is a tool that ultimately allows us to serve others. I'm not sure if I have ever seen anyone grab on to a new concept faster.

The second part of the challenge I made was for Scott to determine how he was going to use his talents and capabilities more fully to serve more people. When I asked him what he really wanted to do, his response was, "To share the platform with you in Las Vegas in January to a room of 10,000 attendees!" As I extended my hand, my response was, "I'll see you there! That will be fun!" In that moment, we both knew it would happen.

The most exciting thing was that we did, in fact, share the platform five months ahead of the original intended date at an event in Toronto. Now that's taking action!

That Sucks – What Now? is a concept that came out of Scott having lived through some unimaginable challenges in life. His willingness to share the stories publicly through this book is admirable, but more importantly, Scott has unearthed some extremely valuable success secrets, techniques, strategies and tips for how to successfully live through the challenges and come out the other side better off for the experiences.

Relying on his faith and using the knowledge and wisdom he has gained over time, he has personally weathered many storms. And now, in this book, he details the real-world solutions to many challenges or difficult times that he shares in his work as a speaker, trainer, and executive coach.

Claiming victory in the good times is easy. Snatching victory from the brink of defeat is much harder but proves that persistence and perseverance will win in the end.

Experience is a great teacher, but typically, it is also a very expensive one. Leveraging Scott's experiences to address the tough issues in your own life is a much more painless and cost-effective way to learn the appropriate behaviors necessary to live a more fulfilled, faithful, and fruitful life.

There is a saying that "when the student is ready, the teacher appears." In many areas of life, I was that teacher for Scott. With his experience of implementing what he has learned from me and from others, and the wisdom he has gained by "living it", Scott can now be your teacher provided you, the student, are ready. I believe that it is no accident that you picked up this book. It means you are ready, and Scott has appeared. Don't waste this opportunity. Make sure to read the whole book and have the intelligence and the courage to implement the wisdom and strategies he shares in your life.

I promise you'll be glad you did!

Jack Canfield

America's #1 Success Coach
Author of The Success Principles™,
Featured Teacher in The Secret, and
Co-Founder of the Chicken Soup for the Soul® Series

PROLOGUE

Consider with me your current quality of life and your business. If you would be given a blank slate and were given both permission and direction to examine and enhance your personal and professional life, what would you choose to address? What areas of your life would you choose to tweak (or overhaul)?

What stressors could you reduce? What benefits could you add? What self-defeating behaviors or situations could you eliminate, change or modify to make your work more pleasant, efficient, effective, and productive, and your personal life more fulfilling?

By combining your personal and business prowess with the strategies, techniques and tips found in this book, potentially you could strengthen your own niche in business, your interactions with co-workers, associates and clients. And perhaps even more importantly, add value, and better differentiate yourself in your field of business.

Some tips may be new to you. However, more than likely, if you have been in business a long time, some tips may be reminders of actions you may have wanted to put into play but were side-lined at the time they came up. Others of you are just starting new entrepreneurial businesses, a new venture or are adapting or modifying your current focus to try a new tack, or to include new, fresh concepts.

All will benefit from the strategies, techniques, tips and interactions you will encounter in these pages, and I welcome your "inspired actions," input and questions. It is together that we can shorten the learning curve and best learn from each other's strengths, challenges, ideas and solutions.

Although business by necessity requires some head-to-head competition, I strongly believe the greater good is for us to work in cooperation and collaboration to benefit and serve each other to enhance the quality of life of all.

It is with this heart that I embark, with you, in this business and life growth endeavor for our greater good.

Scott Schilling

Chapter 1

LIFE HAPPENS TO ALL OF US!

S** Happens!**

S**** happens...and if you're downstream, recognize it will flow in that direction! I'm pretty sure this happens to everyone at some time in their life. Stuff happens and is going to continue to happen.

I learned a concept a long time ago. It states that it is not simply the events that happen in your life which determine the quality of your life. Equally as important is the way you perceive and respond to those events. Together, they create your overall quality of life.

What this concept helps you understand is that you will experience a significant number of events throughout your life. Some experiences will be positive. Some will be uncomfortable. Some experiences will be fabulous, while others less than fabulous. While these events certainly play a significant part in our lives, they are the precursor...the instigator...or the incident that starts the ball rolling.

Far more important than the events themselves, is how you respond to each event. This will ultimately determine the outcomes in your life, and therefore your quality of life. That's why this concept is so important to understand.

I believe that God works for your greater good. These experiences in our lives are designed to have us learn and grow from them.

I encourage you to review this work critically. Take and implement what you like; save the rest for another time.

This book is not meant to chronicle my life, but to share some of the challenges I have faced. More importantly, I'd like to share what I have learned—the processes, techniques, and tips to press through the difficulties that surrounded the challenges.

Rest assured, bad things happen to good people! No one was ever promised a trouble-free life. God *has* promised to be with you through it all. We've been given guidance on how to cope, how to persist, and how to live our best life in the midst of these challenges.

High Intention - Low Attachment

One of the rituals that I find helpful happens before I walk onto the stage, get on a call, or participate in any other event, like training or writing. It allows me to set my mindset on a higher purpose. I take a moment and say the following prayer—

Lord, allow the words that I share here today to positively impact the lives of those reading or hearing this information in one way, shape, or form. Only you know who you sent to read or hear these words. Allow me to do the best I can to deliver those words and be a vehicle and of service to you!

This ritual reminds me that all I can ever control is having a high intention and low attachment. The high intention is centered on the value others will take away. It is a conscious decision to impart only things of high value to the audience. The low attachment is another conscious decision not to be concerned with how the message is received or what becomes the net effect of that message. My intention is to deliver value at all times, through my messages, while not being attached to the actual outcome of how the message is taken or acted upon.

As you can imply from the title of this book *That Sucks…What Now?* much of what we will focus on is what many would suggest are less than favorable events. That being said, the title comes from what I actually said to myself after these unfortunate events took place. *That Sucks* is simply the realization that a particular situation is not exactly ideal.

And the *What Now?* is the fact that it happened, so let's get over it and through with it. No time for a pity party! Let's get to work!

Whether the events are classified as favorable or unfavorable is truly up to the person living the event. Choice is an amazing thing…you have it available to you in every situation and circumstance. What choice will you make for each event you face? Is the glass half-full, half-empty, too small, or twice as big as it needs to be?

The Four Stages of Competence

Let me give you some basis for the information being delivered in this book. There are four stages of competence in all areas of life and business. They reflect an individual's "awareness" intersecting with their "capability".

We all start at the first level of learning where "you don't know what you don't know". From an awareness point of view, you are "unaware" you could possibly know something different than you currently know.

And because of this specific lack of knowing, you are unable to execute the actions required to accomplish a task thus making you "incapable."

The second stage of growth is when "you know you don't know". You have the "awareness" that additional knowledge is available but haven't taken the actions necessary to personally gain that knowledge. You are still "not capable" of accomplishing a specific task but recognize you could if you chose to gain the knowledge necessary.

The third stage of learning is when "you know that you know." You are "aware" there is additional knowledge available to you. You have taken the appropriate actions toward learning the knowledge and are thus "capable" of accomplishing the task.

When there are specific learning points or pieces of information that you really need to learn and embody yourself, they will be delivered from stage three, so you can learn and know them as well! You will become both "aware" and more "capable" by absorbing and implementing this information. The best place to teach is from stage three.

The fourth stage is when the task at hand becomes "second nature" and you "know that you know" how to accomplish the task being "capable," without even thinking about how to do it, and while being able to accomplish another task at the same time.

I share this with you because the place to model the desired result is from stage four. There will be times when I am sharing my experiences, more than likely, from stage four, "second nature".

To show your proficiency and excellence, you should have your actions "grooved" for success in all areas of life and business.

Your Attitude Not Aptitude Will Determine Your Altitude!

Your attitude is a way of thinking or feeling about someone or something. Typically, your attitude is reflected in your behavior.

You may have noticed when a person has a positive attitude. Many times, you can easily tell this by their actions. You might have brought it to another person's attention by saying things like, "I love your can-do attitude!" or, "You never have a bad day!" This a myth by the way—we all have bad days—it simply becomes a matter of whether you show it or not.

While most times you can easily recognize a positive attitude, I'm going to suggest, that virtually every time, you can recognize a person with a negative attitude.

The entirety of their non-verbal communication gives it away.

Notice when they:

- Slouch,
- Move slowly, if at all,
- Have a frown on their face,
- Focus on the negative.

The interesting thing about attitude, is that it is 100 percent in your control. Decide who you want to be.

Do you want to be…

- the person who lights up a room or,

- the person who sucks the life out of it?

One of the intentional practices that has helped to accelerate my career is after interacting with others, I make sure to leave them better off than when I arrived.

To accomplish this intention, it's key to understand what's important to the other person. It's also vital to determine the benefits they will derive from their interaction with you.

More importantly, if it is within your power to deliver their desired benefit, do so. Become known as the person who is always there for others, is dependable, and will do what's possible to brighten their day.

Not long ago, I asked the person I was meeting with how I could be of service. His response was, "It would be great to be on some big stages." I immediately picked up my phone and dialed a promoter I have worked with for years. I told him about the friend I was meeting with, shared his credentials, and suggested he would be a great addition to one of the promoter's upcoming events. In a matter of minutes, my friend was booked on one of the promoter's big stages for an upcoming event. Done!

Everything in Life Begins with a Decision

Have you reached the point where you've just *had it?* You know, where enough is enough. You look at yourself in the mirror or look at the numbers in your bank account and ask yourself, *how did I get this way?* And more importantly, *what the heck am I going to do about it?*

Or, are you dragging your tush? Just not where you'd like to be? Are you just doing the same old, same old or bare minimum to get by? Are you as uninspired as you can possibly be and yet you know deep down inside, you're better than this?

Millions of people around the world are asking the same questions and reaching the same conclusions. They are realizing their personal breaking points. Many times, these breaking points are held internally and never disclosed to the outside world. It's painful, really painful if you'd truthfully admit it. Things like excess weight, a lack of money, despising a job, tolerating unfulfilling relationships, and having no spiritual foundation affects people far more than most people are willing to acknowledge. It was that way for me. It's so easy to laugh it off or justify exactly why it has reached the point it has reached.

The bottom line is pretty simple.

You are not going to have the quality of life you were intended to have if you continue to allow these paralyzing situations to remain. If you don't achieve a reasonable level of proficiency in each area of your life, *it might just be time to reinvent yourself.* That is not meant to scare you or be judgmental in any way. It's just a fact. How do I know? I lived, having deficiencies in one area or another, for the first 60 years of my life!

The good news is that you, and those you love around you, can do something about it. You can't magically remove the effects of the bad or lack of decisions in the past, but you can start fresh, from wherever you are in your life right now, and live the rest of your life as the new inspired you.

The power in making your decision is amazing—it puts your higher source in motion. For me, that higher source is God and Jesus Christ. For you, that might be the Universe, Buddha, Allah, or whomever you have faith and belief in as your higher source of power. Most importantly, it puts you into motion!

The bottom line here is that nothing is accomplished without action. As Napoleon Hill stated in the book, *Think and Grow Rich,* you must be decisive in nature! Make a decision or don't make a decision—not making a decision is utlimately a decision. Have you made a decision yet?

Can it be that simple? Yes! It's not necessarily easy, but it is simple! The word decision comes from the Latin root *decidere* or *to cut away from.* We have to cut ourselves off from our previous path to make room for the modifications and improvements necessary to create what we really want to accomplish in life. How do I know this to be true? By living it daily in so many ways. Let me share some.

Before my beautiful and lovely wife, Peggy, and I were married, we made the decision to experience a happy, fulfilling marriage and that we were going to be married forever. Previously, both of us had unsuccessful marriages and neither of us ever wanted that to happen again.

To insure neither of us ever had to experience the pain and consequences of an unfulfilled marriage again, we sat, talked, and made a conscious joint decision that we would do what it takes to be married forever. By *cutting off* the possibility of anything other than a successful, loving, and wonderful marriage, we are now living that quality relationship today. On November 25th, 2019 we celebrated 24 fabulous years!

One of the initial benefits of making that decision to be married forever was the freedom it gave us. Freedom—huh? You see, by making that original decision, it freed us up from having to make certain choices in the future. Our path was already set. Yours can be, too!

Making this first decision predetermines so many other potential decisions down the road. When you are going to be married forever, you automatically do the things necessary to accomplish that goal. More importantly, you don't do the things that are not going to keep you happily married.

Below are helpful tips that worked for us stepping into our successful marriage:

- Show your love in the five love languages Dr. Gary Chapman suggests. This includes words of affirmation, giving compliments and sharing words of encouragement.
- Spend quality time together, sharing, listening to each other, and participating in meaningful activities.
- Give gifts, as in sending flowers or other visual symbols of love.
- Provide acts of service by doing things willingly for each other and create some amazing results.
- Exchange physical touch, from simple touch to greater intimacy.

Once Peggy and I made the decision to be together forever, caring for each other beyond the call became the standard operating procedure. God, our Higher Source, delivered what we had been really clear on creating for our lives—a magnificent marriage!

A while back, I hit the big 5-0. With all the horror stories you hear from so many people, who would have thought this event was going to be this great! I did, for one, because I decided to make it great. Recognizing that I wasn't in the best shape of my life, although round is technically a shape, I didn't have the fitness or health plan in place to allow me to do what my heart truly desired. I wanted to inspire and empower others to accomplish everything they wanted in their lives. This way, they could share their blessings with so many others in need of daily inspiration.

In short, I recognized it would be hard to fulfill my passions if I was dead. While that statement may be a little dramatic, it's also very true. With that, the decision was made to improve the quality of my health through fitness. Experts were sought out, their guidance was put into place, the plan was executed and here I was, on my way to total lifetime fitness.

In only eight months, I lost 77 pounds of fat, gained 12 pounds of muscle for a 65-pound net weight improvement. Please understand, I never set out to lose weight. I aimed to be fit for the rest of my life. This decision led to acting as fit people act and doing activities fit people typically will do.

The exciting byproduct of becoming healthy is you lose weight because you work out like fit people workout, you eat like fit people eat, and you care for your body like fit people do. My energy level has skyrocketed and more importantly, I have become an inspiration to at least 50 close friends that figured out if I could do it, they could do it, too!

One last fabulous byproduct of becoming fit, beyond feeling great, is that my beautiful wife, Peggy, feels even greater pride in our relationship. From what she has said, I'm looking better than I did when I was 30.

You cannot and will not lose weight or get into better physical shape until you first decide to do so. Once the decision is made and your actions start to reflect this, your Higher Source will support your desires and deliver the resources necessary to accomplish greater health and fitness. Again, is it easy? Maybe not easy, but it is simple. The right decisions will lead you to the information you'll need to set your inner guidance on track. Your internal GPS device will go where you want to go. Choose your destination, plug in your internal GPS or higher source, and be ready to take off!

Let's look at the business and financial realm. Fifteen years ago, I was dead-ended in a corporate job that anyone would love to have. As the Vice President of Sales and Marketing, I ran the sales force, created the programming, and ran the operations for the vast majority of the company. The problem came, that the harder I worked, the more work I created for myself—and I didn't get paid anything in addition to what I was already receiving.

Sound familiar? You make a decent living, but you are not fulfilled or making the impact in the world that matches the talents God gave you. Time to reinvent!

I made the decision to follow my heart and passion to become a professional speaker, author, and streetwise sales consultant. This allowed my capabilities and talents God blessed me with, to be used to a far greater extent. What an amazing feeling to share those talents and to share the knowledge I received from my mentors who imparted their genius to me. Combining that knowledge with my own experiences and my desire to constantly be learning, has allowed me to help so many others. Now, that's fulfillment!

An amazing thing happens when you follow your heart and passions. The rewards for your efforts seek you out! In the past 15 years, I have written 14 books, have two more in the process, have spoken over 4,500 hours on platforms—and, oh yeah—my income has quadrupled!

The true joy in this success was launching my first book, *Talking with Giants! (TWG) Powerful Leaders Share Life Lessons*, in 2007. *Talking with Giants!* is the work that came out of my daily morning proclamation:

I am attracting into my life everything that I need to cause over $100 million in charitable giving!

As I developed that proclamation a number of years ago, I had no clue how it was going to happen. But, as I say in my presentations, when you have a big enough *what*, and you have a strong enough *why*, the *how* shows up! You can attract everything into your life you desire once you gain clarity and release it to your higher source to fulfill. To help accomplish your goals, please visit *www.TalkingWithGiants.com* to learn about the brilliance of the Giants, and the 21 charities supported by this book.

Even more exciting is that the success of *Talking with Giants!* has encouraged me to write more. It has filled me with even greater hope and inspiration and led me to write my latest and best-selling flagship book entitled, *That Sucks…What Now? (TSWN), Real-World Solutions for Getting Through What You're Going Through! That Sucks…What Now?* teaches individuals like you and organizations like yours how to live life fully and achieve total fulfillment.

I don't share any of what I've accomplished to impress you, but rather to impress upon you that you too, can have anything in life you desire once you make the decision to create what you truly want. Obviously, you have to take other actions after the initial decision to accomplish these wants and desires. The exciting part is that, by taking this first action—making a decision—you put your higher source into motion towards accomplishing your goals. One thing is abundantly clear. Without making that first decision, nothing will happen.

A long time ago, someone told me that, "As the chooser, we have the choice to choose, but once that choice is chosen, the choice now controls the chooser!"

No matter where you are in your life, you made the choice to be there some time ago. By reading this book, you can now make the choice as to where you are going to be today, tomorrow, and the rest of your life. What's it going to be? Are you going to say, "Gee, I'm glad I did!" or, "Darn, I wish I would have!"

Live the life of your dreams and imagination—decide to go for it and create the very best life for you!

Engage in Life Fully

It is evident that, once you have a desire to live life fully in all areas, it isn't going to be easy and it isn't for the faint of heart. When you venture out and engage in many of the adventures life has to offer, you'll quickly experience quite the gambit of possibilities.

My desire is for the material in this book to help guide you, give you insight, and hopefully shorten the learning curve so that you can push through challenges in your life easier, quicker, and with less pain.

You can persist. There is hope in the midst of challenge, and your story can and will be an inspiration to others to help them fight through what they come up against. You are powerful and have every right to live full-out.

We live in the most amazing times ever! My wish for you is that you experience every bit of it fully. Let me repeat—Bad things happen to good people. So do good things! You deserve everything that life has to offer. One way to achieve this is to recognize some of the things you may come up against along the way, and the processes to address and handle them appropriately.

One of the early lessons I'd like to share is a concept I learned from one of my mentors, Jack Canfield. It was the concept of:

Growth = Awareness + Inspired Action

This formula has been invaluable to me throughout the years. It basically says that if we have a desire to grow (Growth), the first thing we have to do is to recognize areas we can grow in. Learning more about these areas allows us to become aware of them (Awareness). Learning about them itself is not enough. After we learn or have a new awareness that we can grow into, we have to do something about it (Inspired Action). We have to take action toward that new awareness, and only then will we experience growth.

Life's Most Stressful Events

You fully *know* many or most of the particular stressors currently impinging on your life or business. You can make your own list. For the moment, consider anything in your life that has or imminently will create a sense of overwhelming, intrusive, or persistent and pervasive stress. These areas especially must be examined and acted upon to provide you with crucial emotional, psychological, and physical well-being.

Particularly difficult life events might include personal illness, injury, pain, suffering, the death of a spouse or a loved one, a job change, demotion, firing, being required to move to another city, marriage, separation, divorce, pregnancy, birth of a child, raising children, or getting into trouble with drugs, alcohol, pornography, physical and emotional abuse, or even imprisonment.

Life events which can bring great blessings, also frequently bring great stress, sometimes for only your knowing!

But frequently it is the relatively smaller, irritating things, repetitive issues or interactions, or doubt, lack of decisions, timing, or direction which cause great stress, worry and wakeful nights. Again, start with examining the problem, becoming aware of the issues surrounding the problem, and then taking inspired action to address the issues and decrease your stress. You will be amazed at what you can accomplish if you push through with a can-do attitude. That will be different for each of you. Integrity, happiness, peace and joy are all available to you to live your best life possible.

In working to ensure you get the greatest value from this material, a fair amount of research and study has gone into this book. While it is evident that there are many more events and issues that can cause us stress throughout life, it makes sense to share some potential stressors to give you a foundation for the rest of what is coming up throughout this book.

I have been blessed to be on this planet for quite some time now. By the sheer number of years, I have personally dealt with a number of the top stressors. While I haven't encountered them all, I can verify that the ones I have already lived through have created some great challenges through the years.

Earlier in my life, I experienced the pain of divorce and what it was like to have your kids grow up away from you. I lost my dad in 1996, my mom in 2014, followed closely by my brother in 2015. Losing a family member is never easy.

In college, while playing football at the University of Iowa, a time that produced some of the fondest memories of my life, I suffered a completely severed Achilles tendon on my right foot. I was told I would never play sports again, walk without a limp, or be able to participate in many activities. I came back and accomplished all those things.

As a byproduct of having my Achilles tendon surgically repaired, I became addicted to morphine, Demerol, codeine, and valium. The doctors stair-stepped me down from drug to drug until I went off the valium cold-turkey, something I wouldn't wish on anybody! Because of that entire experience, I have a far better understanding of the opioid crisis today and how insidious it truly is for so many. My heart goes out to all those people whom opioids trap.

I've also lived through a full-blown cerebellar stroke. The multiple blessings after my stroke are many, including *no* residual effects. Injury and significant illnesses are no joke!

I was fortunate enough to get remarried to the wonderful and beautiful, Peggy Emerton-Schilling. Without what I learned from my previous marriage and divorce, we would have never made it to nearly 25 years and counting.

And while I was never dismissed from work, I chose to change professions, going out speaking, training, coaching, and consulting for the last 15 years. If you have not developed the ability to adapt and reinvent, now would be the perfect time to learn.

Chapter 2

YOUR RESPONSE IS TOTALLY UP TO YOU

How Do People Respond to Change?

As you become more aware of the events in your life, I bet you have gained clarity on some things that either you or someone you know has been going through or may have gone through. You may even have a better understanding of some of the actions that were taken. Hopefully, this has increased your compassion and desire to appreciate every situation you, or a loved one, has experienced.

This will be said multiple times throughout this book, but as studies have shown, repetition is the mother of learning, so I will keep saying it. What ultimately matters most, is how people respond to various issues and events that happen in their lives. Although self-doubt and potential self-sabotage will show their ugly heads to you at some point or another, what will be your response? When this happens, you are going to have to reinvent yourself. You are going to get turned down or turned away from doing something. The key is becoming your own biggest cheerleader versus your biggest internal critic.

Let's say you're at a honky-tonk here in Texas and you see someone across the dance floor you want to dance with. You saunter over and ask them to dance and they say no. Many are crushed by such a rejection. Except, it's only a rejection if *you* classify it that way!

Think about it…you weren't dancing. And you're still not dancing. Your life did not get worse! It may not have gone as you thought it might, but only you can turn that event into a negative event. Maybe that person didn't know how to dance. Or they were already with someone else who just stepped away. Regardless, you have to believe in *you*!

It's not what anyone else says to you that counts, it is ultimately what you say to yourself when they stop talking. Other people's opinions are none of your concern. Another way of saying this is, "It's not what people call you…It's what you answer to!"

Far too often, people tend to adopt a negative behavior in attempting to cope with the new reality in their lives. Let's take a quick look to see if you can identify with any of the following.

Playing the Victim – One way to recognize people falling into victimhood is by what they are saying. It might sound something like, "Why me? Why is this happening to me? Why doesn't this happen to_____? Why am I so unlucky? This just isn't fair!"

Sorry, I hate to be the bearer of bad news…life is not always fair! These things are happening to you and many times, you had some part in creating or allowing it to happen to you.

A great way to get yourself out of this is by taking 100 percent responsibility for *everything* that happens in your life. Yep…the one common element in everything that happened to you or through you is...*you*!

When you take responsibility for everything, you actually take back any power you have given up to anyone or anything else. It is truly invigorating…give it a whirl!

Expressing Your Frustration as Anger – Too many people feel so hurt by a particular situation that they lash out physically at the person they feel caused the situation. They may even take it out on a wall or some inanimate object.

Punching a wall or another person is definitely not the best way to let go of frustration. There are other more productive ways to let off steam without creating yet another negative issue that will have to be dealt with.

If physical activity is how you choose to release stress, go for a run! Engage in a sport or do something physical you enjoy. A certain amount of anger is part of our fight or flight response. An abnormally high amount of anger is not good for you or anyone around you. Seek professional guidance if you feel your anger is uncontrollable.

Playing the Shame Game – People often go from being their own internal critic progressing to an internal character assassin. "Why am I so stupid? Why did I make such a dumb mistake? Only I could be that dumb!"

Quite frankly, there is no place for blame, shame, or justification in your responses. Blame suggests someone else is the cause. Shame suggests you are the cause. And justification suggests that there is a good reason this happened this way, so let me explain!

While none of the three should be a consistent answer, shame is probably the toughest to refrain from. The reason is simple. You eventually end up beating up on yourself! Life has enough challenges without you not being on your own side.

If you want to take a stance on anything, become your number one encourager! You were uniquely and wonderfully designed. Recognize this fact and be proud of who you are and all you've become!

Becoming Depressed – Becoming depressed can be a very real and threatening reality. While empathizing with those who fall into depression, I'm fully aware that it robs you of all the good the world has to offer.

I'm not a big fan of medication when to comes to treating depression or virtually any other ailment known to man. I understand that in extreme cases, medication can help start the recovery process. More importantly, it seems prudent to address the root cause of the depression and use other methods to get on the road to recovery.

Choose the things that bring joy into your life. Associate with the people that lift you up, not tear you down. Engage in activities that raise your endorphin levels and allow your body to thrive.

Ultimately, the only thing that heals the body is the body itself or the power that built the body! We were all designed to live at equilibrium, a perfect balance. Find things that encourage you and steadily do more of them until you feel better!

Turning to Drugs, Alcohol, or Some Other Escape – Many times, the pain becomes seemingly too great and the desire to numb out the pain comes into play. Drug or alcohol addiction are tough to successfully overcome. Often, people fool themselves into believing they are able to quit at any time or limit the amount they consume when in reality, it's a very slippery slope.

Use and abuse of drugs and alcohol by teens is very common and can have serious consequences. In the 15 to 24-year-old age range, 50 percent of deaths from accidents, homicides, and suicides involve alcohol or drug abuse. Drugs and alcohol also contribute to physical and sexual aggression such as assault or rape.

While it can be tempting to try a drug or any addictive activity for the first time, it's all too easy for things to go south—especially in the case of drug and alcohol abuse.

Committing Suicide – We have an epidemic going on today with our teens and adults, business people, and military veterans. At this time, our nation is recording an average of 22 military veterans committing suicide each and every day. Many of these suicides are traced back to PTSD or post-traumatic stress disorder. If this is you, please consider visiting www.Mission22.com for ongoing support.

It's almost unthinkable that this group of brave men and women who have gone into the world and defended our liberty and freedom are coming back home and losing this battle. All who have benefited from their service should rally to play a part in addressing and solving this issue.

Among many others, I applaud people like Dave Vobora, the founder of the Adaptive Training Foundation (ATF), here in Dallas, Texas. ATF works with military veterans who have not only fought for our freedom but have also lost limbs or suffered grave injuries. Please support the work and the assistance for those who deserve our thanks. At https://AdaptiveTrainingFoundation.org, you can find ways to support the organization and its efforts for our veterans.

Throwing in the Towel – This is the ultimate give-up. People lose hope and decide it isn't worth it. They believe it's too much to handle, that life is just out to get us, and the best strategy is to quit and stop attempting altogether. They're done!

This is the only time that failure is even a possibility. Until you make a decision to quit and stop trying, everything up to that point is simply a learning event and an opportunity for improvement. Just because the actions taken didn't accomplish what you thought would be accomplished, doesn't mean they were not valuable.

As long as there is breath in your lungs, your heart is beating, and your mind is available to learn, life goes on. Nobody ever said life was going to be easy, although it can become easier. We all face adversity, have tough times, and come against things we would prefer not to come against.

You are much stronger than you think, more resilient than you know, have much more capability than you've given yourself credit for, and have a destiny ahead of you closer than you realize. Get back in the game and go for the glory!

Take 100 Percent Responsibility for Everything

Identifying the ways people typically respond to life's challenges made me think of another great piece of education I had learned years earlier. In Jack Canfield's book, *The Success Principles*™, he encourages us to take 100 percent responsibility for our lives. That's right. You are responsible for *everything*. It is now up to you to do something about it.

The minute you take full responsibility for all your challenges, you become empowered with the ability to do something about them. As a 92-pound child in first grade, I made the choice to eat too much of the wrong types of food. Nobody forced me or fed me with a slingshot from across the room. Nobody forced me to stop at Wendy's for a frosty or at the local pub for a beer on the way back to the hotel after speaking. Nobody told me to make some of the business decisions I've made. Nobody, that was, except me!

When you take back control of your life, whether through fitness or any other area that is not exactly the way you want it, you can make anything happen. And you are responsible! You hold all the power! Why would you want to give it away to anyone or anything? Taking 100 percent responsibility is empowering to say the least!

In fact, you may want to play the responsibility game. In order to live above the line and take 100 percent responsibility for everything in your life, you must eliminate the three pillars of irresponsibility. They are *blame, shame,* and *justification.* Blame is when you say it is someone else's fault or responsibility. Blame is where finger pointing is king. Shame is when you say you're not smart enough or don't have the ability to. Poor little you! And justification or reasons, are simply excuses. Everything can be justified if you work at it hard enough. It's called *spin*!

When we blame, shame, or justify, we completely give up our own power to maintain control of the situation. Why in the world would you want to do that? We need to work toward a world of more personal integrity and calling it like it is. Learning this lesson has proven to be a significant turning point for me to have a much more fulfilling and happy life. Taking responsibility, saying *no* to certain situations and realizing that something had to be done was liberating!

The best part of figuring out the various issues I faced was that it became a baseline to work from. Something could be done about it. For example, I'm truly convinced that no one wants to be overweight and out of shape. Nobody would purposely want the side effects or potential diseases that come along with it. So many times, it is something that kind of creeps up on you due to a lack of awareness. Once people become aware, they become overwhelmed. Individuals become scared and give up before they ever start to do something about it. They give their power away to their lack of fitness. The problem is that their lack of fitness bleeds over into all other aspects of life, whether you want to admit it or not. Balance is balance and if your physical state isn't right, it will cause strain elsewhere.

Living a Life with No Regrets

I want to set the stage with an article. This article was recently published by a nurse who spends time with patients on their deathbed. She detailed the top five regrets people have shared with her before their passing. Let's examine them counting backwards from number five and ending with number one.

Number five of the top five regrets of people on their deathbeds was, *I wish I let myself be happier.* If you're happy, look in the mirror and tell yourself this! We live in a serious world. I think, too serious. My lovely wife, Peggy, and I were out in the backyard just the other night. A bee kept flying around my head…circling like it was lining up for the kill. While I wasn't finding it overly funny at that moment, Peggy was laughing. She was rolling at the faces I was making as I was losing my battle with this stubborn bee.

Later on, when we talked about it further, we both had the opportunity to laugh about it. We were able to make light of how goofy the entire event was. I know for me, if there is ever a time where it feels like I'm up against something or someone, there is nothing better than to look at the lighter side of things. It's one of the reasons I love the movie *Tommy Boy!* It's potentially one of the funniest movies in history.

Number four of the top five regrets of people on their deathbeds was, *I wish I had stayed in touch with my friends.* The beauty of social media makes it possible for us to do just that. Not too long ago, I attended my 40-year high school reunion. Three years prior to this event, my old friends and I started connecting through social media. First, one person posted our eighth-grade football team photo online and asked everyone to identify the players.

Not long after that, someone else posted our ninth-grade football team photo. Soon, there were posts of our grade school years, all across the school district. The number of old classmates that started playing along, posting messages, and reconnecting with each other was amazing. By the time we actually had the reunion, we had hundreds of classmates and loved ones who joined in the festivities.

Recapturing our youth through the retelling of stories and fun times was truly a blessing. While some may look at social media as a burden and potentially the downfall of our youth today, it can be a great way to rekindle old relationships and stay in touch with those with whom we spent so much time during our formative years.

Number three on the top five regrets list was, *I wish I had the courage to express my feelings*. Being a baby boomer, it seems fairly common in my generation that boomers may not be the best at letting their feelings out. This is probably one of the reasons diseases are so prevalent among us…you have to let things out and let them go!

When my 31-year-old son was only three years old, I remember we visited my dad in the hospital after his triple bypass surgery at age 75. As my dad came out of his anesthesia, he looked up and told me he loved me. That was the first time I recall him being emotional.

Don't get me wrong, my dad was a great man. He worked hard to provide our family with a solid foundation and a great life. He was raised in the depression era. As such, we were raised much the way he was raised. Families loved each other, but typically went without expressing it freely.

That was the moment I decided that my kids and those I loved, would never have to wait to hear how much I loved them! I grew up German and Dutch, so the people who raised me were very strong people. Nevertheless, I was going to tell my kids that, of course, I loved them!

Tell people you love them. I once had a near death experience and fortunately, I came out the other side. You can never express how much you care for another too often. I would encourage you to tell and show those you care about, how much you really do care for them. Express this to them frequently and don't wait for them to tell you first. There's a little unsolicited relationship advice for you.

The number two regret on the top five list of regrets was, *I wish I didn't work so hard*. Work is a wonderful thing and we all basically have to perform one type of work or another. My encouragement to you would be to work smarter, not harder. You know I'm very blessed. I've written checks to nineteen mentors over my career. If you want to become better in a specific area of life, the chances are you do not have to reinvent the wheel. It has already been invented, and someone has developed a pretty solid working model for you to use.

The only thing I ever said upfront to every one of my mentors was *give me everything you got,* and I promise I won't keep it for myself. Share all the expertise and knowledge you have gained in your pursuit to greatness, and I will share it with my students and those whose lives I will touch, impact, and change. That's all we can do. Leave it all on the playing field once we give it everything we have!

And the top regret of those lying on their deathbed was, *I wish I had the courage to live a life true to myself, not the life others expected of me.* Wow! Can you believe that? The number one thing that most people regret at the end of their lives is that they did not live their truth! They did not live out their dreams, their visions, their destiny. Instead, they allowed the life that others dictated to them to become their own.

Do you understand you are uniquely built to be the one and only you? Why are you working so hard to fit in when you have been distinctively designed to stand out?

You were a winner from the beginning when you beat out 15 million other sperm that could have fertilized your egg. Or, you are the egg that was fertilized out of the vast number of eggs possible. Every bit of you has been designed for greatness. You have been built in the image of your Creator…and He doesn't make junk!

The material we're about to dive into comes from years of experience. Much of it is personal. Yep, I actually lived this stuff! Other stories that will be passed along are from close friends who encountered events on their paths throughout their lives.

I'm sharing some very personal experiences, not because I want you to know about the events. Rather, I share the information to give you a foundation for why certain decisions were made and why certain actions were taken. And oh, by the way, I am not pretending to have all the answers. The one thing I have learned throughout my life and all the events I've lived through is, seeking wise council is a sign of strength, not weakness!

All of us have moments where we share this fairly common response... *That Sucks...What Now?*

Far too often, something happens in life and many are quick to classify what just happened as an unfortunate incident. Is it really? Is what just happened to you an unfortunate incident? Or is it a life-defining moment?

I'd like to share the following story to tie in what we've discussed so far, with a real-life event. While I share things about me, this is really not just about me, but much bigger things. Throughout this book, I'm going to share some things that I've never shared before, from the stage or in a book. Thinking about it, I don't know that I've shared this with even a handful of people, so we have to get on with it before I change my mind! One of the keys to go from simply surviving to absolutely thriving is to be real, raw, and relevant. That means you have to be authentic and vulnerable. Yes, it's scary—but, as they say—it is what it is!

Chapter 3

REAL-WORLD EVENTS CREATE REAL-WORLD SOLUTIONS

Good Morning - This is Your Wake-Up Call!

It's a cool, crisp, and beautiful morning in sunny Los Angeles. It's probably about 64 degrees, not a cloud in the sky, and a lovely Sunday. It's the perfect day to enjoy the day off, go to church with friends, take part in a wonderful service at Matthew Barnett's Angelus Temple, head over to the Dream Center, and then have a pleasant lunch with friends.

Services at the Angelus Temple are inspiring to say the least. There's great music, worship, and Matthew Barnett delivers thought-provoking messages for churchgoers from all walks of life. In fact, those enrolled in the Dream Center program fill entire sections in the worship center.

While everything around us is comforting and peaceful, something just doesn't feel right.

After the service, we had the honor of joining Pastor Matthew back in a green room to meet staff, other attendees, and learn more about the programs and offerings of the church. On the other side of the room is singer Katy Perry's mom and dad, who dropped by to thank the pastor and share a kind word.

Something is definitely not right, but what is it? I can't put my finger on it. I drink a bottle of water, since I'm so thirsty. Maybe it's because I hadn't had breakfast. I have some almonds, and then a little bag of beef jerky. I'm working to feel normal. But, I don't! I come back to the conversation at hand.

"Would you like to tour the Dream Center?" It's actually the old Rampart Hospital from the 1970s television show, *Emergency,* that aired from 1972 to 1979.

I reply, "Absolutely!"

Founded in 1994, The Dream Center is a volunteer-driven organization that finds and fills the needs of over 80,000 individuals and families each month. In fact, 734 former pimps, prostitutes, drug dealers, and drug addicts live in the remodeled hospital turned Dream Center. These residents are part of a discipleship program that welcomes them, educates them, and helps those with a desire to improve their lives do just that.

The mission of the Dream Center is impressive. It is to reconnect isolated people to God and a community of support. They do this by providing human services that address immediate and long-term needs in the areas of homelessness, hunger, poverty, addiction, education, and human trafficking. *Wow!*

And their vision to accomplish this is inspiring! They are building a community of resilient people whose lives have been redeemed by God's love. The lives they change are not the only examples of God's power to restore broken lives. These men, women, and families go on to share that love with others, passing on the hope they have been given, and making transformation possible for others.

This work literally transforms neighborhoods, providing hope and inspiration to all the lives they touch. *Wow again!*

"Let's head to the roof so you can see some of the breadth of the efforts and results. The view is breathtaking!" We all headed up to the roof. The panoramic view of the city was incredible.

Everyone should be fortunate enough to have this experience, to see firsthand what can be accomplished with a dream, a vision of what can be, and the actions required to make it happen. This was truly memorable!

It was time for lunch, so we decided to go to the Universal City Walk. There were all sorts of great spots there. We headed back to the hotel so we could take the shuttle over to the Universal City Walk. This would only take a few minutes.

As we exited the shuttle and walked about 20 feet, it happened. My legs stopped working! I looked down and realized I couldn't feel either leg from just above the knees down. I'm suddenly standing on tingly stumps. As that realization comes to my consciousness, I started to become disoriented. Fortunately, there was a railing next to me. I grabbed on quickly.

Walking with seven people at the time, three of them were doctors... Was this a coincidence? I think not! One of the doctors spun around to see what was happening and asked me for my phone number. I replied with my number and then said, "Why would you ask me that? Can't you see I can't walk?"

I was suddenly cold, pale, clammy, sweating profusely, disoriented and more. I had four of the five indicators that I was in the middle of having a full-blown cerebellar stroke!

God Here – You Awake?!

If you think I wasn't scared, confused, upset, concerned, and many more emotions filled with all kinds of thoughts, you are wrong. I was terrified in a single instant! My Higher Source most certainly had my attention now! What will it take for you to wake up? While I'll share more of the story of my stroke in a later chapter, I want you to understand how stirred up I was after this event in my life. So many people are asleep and complacent with their lives today. Make sure you are wide-awake and seeing your life clearly for what it is right now.

Defining Moments

Everyone has times in their lives when events, situations, and circumstances can be termed as defining moments. They come in a variety of sizes, shapes, and configurations. So many people who consistently ignore symptoms and red flags find themselves in the heat of situations including divorce, estranged family relations, bankruptcy, hating their jobs, addictions, exhaustion, health issues, weight gain, weight loss, emptiness, and the list goes on.

This is probably not the way you want to come to the realization that things must change. If you want to *be* more, *do* more, and *have* more, you probably need to modify how you are *doing life*.

There are moments and times when you can finally decide for change to happen. Take the fork in the road, turn left, turn right, plow straight ahead, backup, or come to a screeching halt. My question to you is simple. How's what you're doing working for you? More importantly, are you willing to do something about it?

My gut tells me you are, because you've taken the first step by obtaining this book and reading this far. Congratulations! As mentioned earlier, Growth = Awareness + Inspired Action. If you truly want to grow in your life, you must first gain the awareness that there is a new way, place, and method for you to potentially achieve new ground. And then you must take the inspired action to get you there.

I've had many such *events* in my life, and while I'd like to say I *used* them all to their fullest, that would not be truthful. If there is any good news about that, I'm pretty sure I'm not the Lone Ranger here. At first, it's like a gentle tap on your shoulder. If and when it becomes serious enough, it's like a two-by-four to the head and shoulders like in *Tommy Boy*. Now, that's going to leave a mark! Not listening to God, only to have some shocking event happen to me, has helped me come to realize that I am allergic to lightening!

It's also quite frankly one of the reasons for writing this book. It's to give you and those you share this information with the permission that it is okay that you may have misinterpreted those moments or not acted on them as you now wished you had…up until now!

Personally, I've also come to find out that as we grow more mature, we eventually recognize what is truly important in life. It's not just about success anymore, it becomes about significance! Success is about accomplishment and significance is about the meaning behind the accomplishment.

Recently, Brian Fleming, a good friend and a true inspiration in my life, wrote about suffering and significance. Here are two excerpts from his books, *Redeployed: How Combat Veterans Can Fight the Battle Within and Win the War at Home,* and *Never the Same.*

"At all costs, find meaning in your suffering. It's just about the only thing that will pull you through. I've been asked thousands of times over the past decade about how I was able to bounce back so quickly after waking up a bloody mess in a ditch on the side of the road in Kandahar, Afghanistan to being who I am and where I am today. I found meaning in my suffering, plain and simple.

To find it, it had nothing to do with me and everything to do with you. Healing isn't found…by focusing on yourself and your circumstances. It's discovered as you continue to focus on helping other people win their own battles, in spite of the pain you're experiencing. This is the only way I've ever been able to discover a sense of meaning in my most painful experiences and it made the absolute difference in the outcome of my life.

Your perspective is the bridge between your pain and the place you want to be. You have what it takes. Keep moving forward."

Brian, a decorated U.S. Army Veteran and author, is an inspiration to me and so many others. His words and thoughts have helped me realize that it is through helping others that our lives have value. In fact, it is written in Romans 8:28 of the Bible (NIV translation)—

"And we know that in all things God works for the good of those who love Him, who have been called according to His purpose."

The first three words are the key...*and we know*! That's right, we already know deep down inside that everything in our lives is meant for our good. Even though many times, as something happens or when we are in the midst of it, it is not pleasant in the least.

Let's Agree on Perseverance, Hope, and Inspiration

Now, let's focus on a few critical themes which weave throughout the experiences, lessons, observations, and suggestions in this book. These principles are key for you to absorb. I encourage you to implement what can be learned, especially throughout these next pages.

Perseverance

Let's first look at perseverance. If we look at the definition, perseverance is *the continued effort to do or achieve something despite difficulties, failure, or opposition*. Has anybody had difficulties, failure, or opposition in their lives? How about in your business, job, family, or relationships? Unfortunately, most of these difficulties we find ourselves up against are a result of our choices.

Perseverance is *the action, condition, or instance of enduring*. It can be termed as *steadfastness*. It is fighting through when the fight is being lost, even for a moment. Perseverance means being persistent and facing any difficulties that show up unexpectedly. It is not accepting what others may call failure, since there is no failure, but only learning opportunities! Perseverance is pressing on against opposition that doesn't share the vision you have internally.

It's going through things again and again. We all have gone through many things throughout our lives. How many of you have had stuff happen where you actually had to persevere?

The point is, we all have stuff happen to us every minute of every day and it's not about the stuff. *It's what we do about the stuff.* We all are going to come up against something at some time, by choice or by chance. This will cause you, the individual, to have to reinvent a portion or maybe even your entire life or business affairs.

Perseverance is when you are being resolute, dutifully firm, and unwavering in the pursuit of your mission. It's keeping the faith in the face of all adversity. Be the powerhouse you have been created to be in all that you do. Remember, you're amazing!

As an active participant in life and having the good fortune to surround myself with many excellent human beings, I have studied, learned, and have taught for years what I have found to be the best way to persevere in life. I'll be detailing the process further as you continue on throughout the rest of this book. The good news is, I truly believe it comes down to a simple process that anyone can put into action to live a truly fulfilling life.

Hope

Hope is a feeling of trust in a certain outcome. It is a feeling of expectation and a desire for a certain thing to happen. Hope's strength is the strength of a person's desire. Biblically, it is the confident expectation of what God has promised, and its strength comes from His faithfulness.

Hope is a choice each individual makes to believe in what has yet to come.

Inspiration

Inspiration is a divine influence or action in a person believed to qualify him or her to receive and communicate sacred revelation. It is also the power of moving the intellect or emotions. It is the act of influencing or suggesting opinions.

Inspiration is an inside-out activity. Where extrinsic motivation comes from the outside to motivate your actions, inspiration comes from the inside to inspire your outward actions. Inspiration will continue to fuel you long after your motivation has worn off.

We're All a Compilation of Our Experiences

If you are like most people, you have had plenty of ups and downs, hills and valleys, and good and not as good things happen in your life. All of your experiences work to shape, mold, and refine you. Just like gold, sometimes this takes some pretty intense *fire*! It is the fire that removes the impurities and ultimately helps us to shine even brighter.

If you are reading this now, you have already gone through some of the things that have encouraged you to pick up this book. You are enough…exactly as you are. But I do commend you for your yearning for continual growth. Congratulations on your desire to live more fully!

Keith Cunningham, Author of *Keys to the Vault*

Over the course of my speaking career, I've had the pleasure of sharing the platform with Keith Cunningham on several different occasions. Keith is a marvelous speaker and teacher. He focuses his trainings on how to run your business efficiently and profitably. In his presentations, he talks about developing your business to be the best that it can possibly be. He encourages you to reach your fullest potential and accomplish what you have been put on earth to achieve. This next statement that Keith uttered has become my new mantra. It is simply, *"Hell on earth is meeting the man or woman you could have been!"*

When I first heard Keith say it, it sent a shudder through my body. That is one powerful statement! It seems as if most people sincerely want to be the best they can be deep down inside. Then, somewhere along the way, life happens, and all sorts of great intentions get cast to the side or at the very least, put off for far too long. The great news is that each and every one of us can dust off those ideas and put them back into action. That act alone will provide inspiration to those who witness it.

We all have capabilities far beyond what we use on a consistent basis. With this, we can provide value to at least one other human being on this planet. Everyone knows one thing that someone else doesn't know but needs to know. If you think about it, it's not that hard to be an inspiration to someone else. It just takes a little thought, action, and desire.

Darkness is the Absence of Light
Don't Like the Dark? Be the Light!

Darkness takes over due to the absence of light. Brightness and brilliance, on the other hand, appear as soon as light shines. You, me, we all have the ability to be that light should we choose to do so. Being a light in the darkness is a choice. A great one at that!

Typically, it doesn't take all that much light to dissipate the darkness. Because darkness is absence of light, choose to be a light and shine brightly wherever darkness lurks. Far too many times, it has been said by others, *"I don't have the influence that so and so has. Who is going to listen to me?"*

This is a time when you can refer to those who do have that tremendous reach and impact, and understand why this is their mindset. Mother Teresa put it this way, *"If you can't feed one hundred, feed one!"*

You are powerful! If all you can do is start by helping one, this one thing is certain—the *one* you help out will benefit and appreciate you!

The Starfish Story

The Starfish story has been told repeatedly in personal development circles. Its goal is to encourage others that no matter how many people you touch, your efforts always make a difference.

For those who may not have heard the story, here's a quick version for your consideration.

One day, a man was walking down the beach, when off in the distance, he noticed what seemed to be a young lady jumping and dancing at the waters' edge. As the waves came in, she seemed to rush out into the waves dancing and flinging her arms toward the water.

As the water retreated, she too retreated to the beach, bent down, and repeated her dance into the waves. It was only as the man grew closer that he was able to get a better look at what was actually happening.

As she bent down to pick up something on the glistening sand, he saw that there were what seemed to be endless numbers of starfish that had washed ashore with the power of the waves. They settled on the sand before being washed back into the water. The young lady was picking up one starfish at a time and flinging it back into the ocean.

As he drew even closer, he shouted out to the young woman, "What are you doing? You can't possibly make a difference!" With that, the young woman picked up one more, danced into the water, flung the starfish far out beyond the waves, turned to the man and said, "It made a difference to that one!"

In your story and my story, the unique things in life were not put into our lives by accident. They were put into our lives to serve ourselves and others. It is only through the human experience that we gain our ability and capability to contribute to the human experience of others.

Fame vs. Impact

One more thought to wrap up this chapter comes from a coaching session with Victoria Trabosh. Victoria is one of my wonderful clients. She is also a coach, speaker, and author. The concept of *Fame vs. Impact* came up during one of our coaching calls. We were discussing her desire to have a certain person write an endorsement statement for her upcoming book *Dead Rita's Wisdom*. This is a tremendous book, by the way – please check it out!

As we talked through this situation, Vicky shared her desire to have this endorsement because she felt it could potentially help with the sales of the book. This was a reasonable desire to want to get the endorsement. The value it would provide would allow a deeper delve into the marketplace. The person she wanted to write the endorsement was well-known and had a pretty significant reach.

As Vicky approached this person to write the endorsement, they said, "You write it…and I'll sign off on it!"

Vicky is a tremendously intuitive soul, one of her attributes that makes her such a great coach! Anyway, she didn't like the way it all felt. It seemed disingenuous and this triggered our discussion.

My question to her was, "Are you wanting this endorsement because of the potential fame that could come from selling a significant number of books? Or, are you writing the book because of the potential impact that can be created through the wisdom found within the book?"

Her answer, as I expected knowing her heart was, "Impact! It's about making a difference in the world."

Awesome, great answer. "Then, what's the conclusion?" I asked.

"It doesn't make sense to use this person as an endorser if, in fact, they aren't really taking ownership of the endorsement," she replied. Awesome again!

We talked more about this for a little bit, and it ultimately came down to the thought of the intention behind the endorsement. The motivation in potentially selling more books was one that I classified as fame, whereas Vicky's true intention was that of having impact.

To solidify the point, I asked a couple more questions. "What if you only sell one book, would that be okay?" I was pretty sure Vicky wasn't sure where I was going with this question.

"I wouldn't be at all excited about selling only one," she responded.

"What if that one was to the person who became the next Mother Teresa because of your book?"

"That would be impact!" she said.

"Exactly!"

Here's a thought to ponder. It only takes two, telling two, telling two, telling two, 32 times and we've reached everyone on this planet. Far too many times, people want to create huge impact all at once and aren't willing to *be the light* to the first two!

Hopefully, you will take what you learn throughout this book, put it into action, and do your part in *telling two* to make the world a better place.

So, What Is Legacy, Success, and Significance?

You hear these words all the time. The question is, what meaning do you assign to each of these words?

Through many conversations with people most would consider to be tremendously successful, it is interesting how the conversation twists and turns as the discussion of legacy, success, and significance come up. Each person comes with their own frame of reference. It only seems logical to share some of these different viewpoints.

To help ensure you and all who read this material are on the same page, let's create the definitions we can all agree upon to have an open and valuable discussion when it comes to legacy, success, and significance.

Legacy

Legacy is anything handed down from the past, by will, or bequest. To me, legacy is not simply something you hand down once you have died. Rather, it should be *what you are known for as you live!* In other words, the *past* can be the *immediate past.*

The greatest example of this concept I can think of is Mother Teresa. Here's a woman who spent every day working with the poor, the destitute, and the disadvantaged as a living example of love, joy, peace, patience, kindness, goodness, faithfulness, gentleness, and self-control. We didn't have to wait until she passed to learn of her legacy. She lived it in front of our eyes daily. Mother Teresa was an amazing example of living your legacy!

Legacy is certainly those possessions, concepts, and initiatives that you leave to future generations after you die. But what if people were more conscious of being of service, doing good in the world, and having a far greater impact in the present? Can you imagine how much positive impact could be created around the world?

Living your legacy allows you to not only provide residual benefits to those you want to positively impact in the future. It also allows you to revel in the positive impact you create throughout your lifetime. It is a gift you can give away and still experience yourself. "Legacy is not what you leave *to* someone…it is what you leave *in* someone!"

Success

Success is, that sometimes illusive, many times frustrating, and often times achieved goal for so many. So, what is success? As I talked with many high achievers throughout my career, it became clear that the term, success, has subjective definitions. In exploring the many individual definitions, it is abundantly obvious that success is defined based upon an inward orientation. It is personal and dependent upon what each individual identifies as important.

Some see success as the simple accomplishment of their goals. Others, as the attainment of wealth, prominence, or honors. Interestingly, all these definitions are in essence man-made and many times self-created. It could be said that success is in the eye of the beholder.

Don't get me wrong, the desire to be successful and accomplish many wonderful things throughout your lifetime is admirable. I look at times in my career where certain things were accomplished and considered a huge success. These were very rewarding times. The thing that I find interesting again, in talking with many of whom would be considered high achievers, is that even though they achieved success, there was a hollowness or emptiness attached to the achievement in so many situations.

In fact, upon accomplishing their goals, they immediately established new goals to aim toward. They were constantly striving for the next level and not stopping long enough to enjoy what was just achieved! Many don't even stop long enough to smell the roses once they get the roses. There is nothing wrong with constantly trying to be the best or have more. But when it becomes about the game and not the results of it all, it seems value has been lost where it could have been gained. That's where I believe significance comes into play.

Significance

There have been a number of very learned authors, speakers, trainers, and philosophers who have worked to quantify significance. Personally, with everything I have experienced over my lifetime, I believe understanding how to create a life of significance is extremely important for living a satisfied, happy, and high-quality life.

While significance can mean having importance or something of value, too many times these definitions are again, subjective. When you change the orientation from inward importance to outward benefit, it is amazing how different your view of significance will become.

When looking at significance as it reflects outward, to you, to the world, a certain inner glow takes effect. Significance is the quality of having meaning. It's not simply achieving a goal or something substantial, it's the meaning and importance behind that accomplishment. How will that accomplishment benefit far more people than just you? In essence, the answer will lie in how that accomplishment aligns with your living out your legacy today.

We live in interesting times. Being a baby boomer, many around my age are having a tremendously hard time with the millennial generation. You often hear how entitled millennials feel, that they can't or won't hold down a job, and that it's more about purpose than position.

Generally, for millennials, work is a means to an end. That end is contributing to the greater good! They tend to be more interested in community and social causes versus stomping on top of another to claim the next position up the ladder.

What many baby boomers fail to realize is that what many would call laziness or discontentment, I believe is really the millennials' desire to seek significance and not just success. The part many boomer friends have shared is that it just doesn't seem fair that the millennials wanted significance without having to go through all the struggle we went through "paying your dues." As baby boomers, we realized *we also* wanted significance over success.

Here's the part I find to be extremely exciting. When a baby boomer gets their head straight and understands that millennials actually want to live a life of significance too, the boomers must realize they have the accumulated wisdom that millennials need to be able to fast-track their lives to significance! Mentoring can be established, giving way to a potentially swift and massive impact for the good.

Significance is an inward determination of an outward action. So many times, it comes as a feeling you experience internally for the action taken externally. It is the result of one-to-many or even one-to-one interactions with greater positive results. With success, you may be happy, whereas with significance there is a deeper more heart-felt emotion—Joy! Happy is fun but Joy is endearing.

It is the depth of meaning that makes the difference. In the song, "If Everyone Cared" by Nickelback, they sang it this way—

> *"If everyone cared and nobody cried,*
> *if everyone loved and nobody lied,*
> *if everyone shared and swallowed their pride,*
> *then we'd see the day when nobody died."*

There is apparently a human decency that rises to the forefront when we apply this superior, more profound meaning to our actions and most importantly, to our lives.

Wisdom

> *Wisdom is the Ability to Determine Today*
> *the Consequences of Tomorrow...*

Wisdom is typically gained through experience. Many times, experience is gained through taking actions only to find the results of those actions did not achieve the goal. The reason that many people say wisdom comes with age is because we all have to go through enough things, good and bad, to be able to set up comparisons of successful or unsuccessful outcomes.

Being able to critically evaluate the actions taken and incremental results delivered is key to gaining wisdom. Lessons are lived out and available to us if they are observed and absorbed fully. Removing ego from the equation furthers true humility and the potential of ultimate mastery.

> *True wisdom comes to each of us when we realize how little we understand about life, ourselves, and the world around us.*
>
> *—Socrates*

Personally, I believe that many of the issues and negative events we experience throughout our lives are there to give us the juxtaposition necessary to live a more evolved life. There is a certain truth in saying that wisdom comes from experiencing a breadth of events that each of us have happen to us throughout our lifetime. Embrace the thought that life's events are not happening *to* you but rather happening *for* you! At certain points in your life, you may find that you now have the ability to prevent undesirable consequences from happening, even before they occur. You've learned to act on the wisdom you've gained from prior life experiences.

When we look back at the Bible (Romans 8:28 NIV) and review some of the wisdom that dates back to the Romans, we see that this statement still rings true today—

> *"And we know that in all things God works for the good of those who love Him, who have been called according to His purpose."*

Chapter 4

EVENTS EITHER CHANGE OR DEFINE YOU

Life-Changing Events or Defining Moments?

I was a five-sport athlete in high school. While I was pretty good at all sports, I wouldn't necessarily say I was great at any one of them. The great news was that I was good enough to have the opportunity to play at the next level.

Because of my athletics, I had multiple scholarship opportunities that ranged from junior colleges, to Division 1, 2, and 3 level schools. Seemingly, my best shot came with football. I grew up in Milwaukee, Wisconsin during the days of Marquette University's basketball coach, Al McGuire. Al McGuire took the Marquette Warriors to the NCAA championship in 1977.

And of course, because he was building such an amazing program at Marquette, I went to Al McGuire's basketball camp every summer. For those of you who know me, I'm sure you have always thought I had a basketball body. Yeah? Well, maybe not!

Football became an obvious choice, so I visited Drake University in Des Moines, Iowa. I had the chance to attend the Ivy League of the Midwest and receive a full-ride scholarship at Drake University. Even though few knew about their football program, opportunities existed for me to enroll in this outstanding school and get a scholarship. It was during my official visit at Drake University when the coaches from the

University of Iowa called me and said to stop by Iowa City on the way back to Milwaukee from Des Moines.

So, on the drive back to Milwaukee, we stopped by Iowa City. It was just amazing. Everybody should have to live in Iowa for a period of time. I'm not suggesting forever. I'm just suggesting for any period of time. It's an amazing place.

The coach, Larry Donovan, who was hosting me said that they would love to have me. However, since it was late in the recruiting cycle, I'd have to walk-on. All of their scholarships were already committed. Coach Donovan encouraged me by saying that if I really had the ability that everyone believed I had, then the opportunity to earn a scholarship would happen quickly.

Wow. I had a decision to make. I'd either take a guaranteed scholarship at Drake which was a smaller school with academic prestige, or walk-on at the University of Iowa. Here, I would have to earn my spot among a team full of scholarship players, and with no guarantees. All this happened while I was getting offers from Michigan State and Minnesota, as well as smaller schools.

Growing up in Wisconsin, I didn't even know Iowa existed. Neither the school, nor the state. I had always dreamed of playing at Wisconsin. Unfortunately, the Wisconsin head coach, John Jardine, told me I wasn't good enough to play in the Big Ten. I thought, *Wait a minute! Michigan State, Minnesota, and Iowa are all in the Big Ten!* Although this was the first time I was ever in Iowa, thoughts started running through my head. *This feels right. But how did I get here? Oh, my God! Is this meant to be?* So, I walked on because you know who believed in me? You got it! Me!

That first season, as a walk-on, they put me on every scout team. Basically, this scout team was the meat they threw to the lions during every practice. There were occasions to kick and punt during drills, and this is when I caught my coach's attention. Kicking and punting actually are what ended up paying for my school! As the season ended, and scholarships became available in the new year, my coach called me in to give me the news. I was now on a full ride!

And so, all of a sudden, not only did I walk-on at Iowa, but after one semester, I earned my scholarship. I fought through and I earned it even though there were other players in my position who were already on scholarships. And not only that, as we went into my sophomore season, I earned the starting position. From not knowing where Iowa was a year earlier, to now being able to represent the black and gold proudly, to the 70,000 fans who came to every game—what a feeling!

Our third game of 1977 was the renewal of the Iowa vs. Iowa State series. The schools had not played in 42 years because they hated each other, and I mean *hated*. In their last game, 42 years prior, there was such a big blowout that the game was discontinued. As we were coming up to that big day, the pressure on both sides was mounting. We were going to be on national television for the first time ever. Ara Parseghian was going to be commentating on our game. This was big time! The other pressure packer? The point spread was two. Now, why is that important? Because I was the kicker!

Oh man, the pressure. The renewal of the rivalry after 42 years, and here I am. Somehow, I'm the kicker and all the pressure was on me. You know what I did? My buddy Steve Ewalt, who played on the golf team, and I went to Finkbine Golf Course and played a round of golf Thursday morning.

Yes, I went to the golf course. I had to get away. So, I got away with Steve and began to relax as we golfed. Once we came to the 12th green and finished the hole, we noticed that the 13th tee box was down a fairly steep hill. It had rained that morning, and we had decided to take a golf cart out to save our legs. We didn't want to burn our legs out. As we came down the hill, the cart started going too fast.

I tapped on the brakes. In doing so, the brakes locked, and the cart started sliding, except it also turned sideways. Suddenly, the cart began sliding with me on its low side, all the way down the hill. We were going way too fast and I saw a berm at the very bottom. The wheels caught on the berm, and the cart abruptly stopped and started to roll over. Having no control, I was ejected full spread eagle on the low side with my right foot, which was my kicking foot, hanging back.

Because the cart was starting to roll over, Steve intuitively saw what was going to happen and he leaned with all his weight on the high side to keep the cart from rolling over me. When he leaned over, it caused the cart to crash into its suspension. One tragedy averted. But, wait! There's more!

As the cart bounced on its suspension, it went straight up and toward my kicking foot, which was now dragging. As the cart came crashing down, the sharp edge of the cart came down and completely severed my Achilles tendon on my kicking foot. It also broke the bones behind it. This just about cut off my foot. Well, at least that's how it felt.

Lying face down in the dirt, I dug my toe into the ground to hopefully stabilize my foot for a moment. Believe it or not, what actually hurt worse was my jaw. When the cart hit my foot, the reflex action caused my leg to coil away from the cart, which in turn shot my knee straight up into my jaw. I thought I had broken my jaw. This was my immediate concern. The body is an amazing thing. It's only able to feel one acute severe pain sensation at a time!

Now that everything had stopped for a second, Steve joked and said, "Come on! Get back in the cart. I'm even par!" I tried to get up and put some weight on my right foot.

I said, "No, man. I think I sprained my ankle." I put a little more weight on and said, "No, I think I broke my ankle!" That's when I looked back and saw a two-by-two-inch hole in the back of my foot with something sticking out of it. That was my Achilles tendon. It was then that I buried my head in the dirt and said, "Call an ambulance. I'm going to have surgery this afternoon, and I'm out for the season. I'm in deep s***!"

The reporting of my injury hit all the press outlets. It made *The Daily Iowan*, the local Iowa City newspaper. To this day, one of the hardest parts of reliving this story is reading Coach's words. "He's the best field goal kicker we've had in a long time." Not only did I let myself down, I let my coach and teammates down.

When I arrived at the hospital, Dr. John Albright, our team doctor said, "Scott, I just want you to know, you'll probably never play sports again.

You'll probably have issues with this for the rest of your life. And, you'll probably never walk without a limp."

I replied while in a drug-induced state, "Sew me up, Doc! I'll be back!"

The good news is that one of us was right, me! Was this a life-changing event? Absolutely! More importantly, was it a defining moment? Yes, *absolutely*!

To this day, 40 years later, my right calf is an inch and a half smaller than my left because of the atrophy and other issues I went through during my rehabilitation. I continued rehabilitation and was working out 75 days later. I was kicking footballs in Spring practice. I earned my starting spot back within months. I rejoined my teammates, Bobby Stoops, Andre Tippet, and Jay Hilgenberg who all went on to have great coaching or NFL careers.

I've won ten racquetball championships since. I've also had four NFL tryouts. I came back and played. And, by the way, the Iowa vs. Iowa State renewal made it into *Sports Illustrated*. Probably not the way I wanted to make *Sports Illustrated*, but then again, why not? For one, this man, legendary Coach Hayden Fry, came to Iowa. And then, I was told I'd never play again. I'd never walk right. I'd never return to football, and they were dead wrong. Because I did come back and had the honor of playing for Coach Fry.

This is not meant to impress you, rather it is meant to impress upon you that you are wonderfully made and infinitely capable. You have greatness within you. It is, however, up to you to let it out! As Henry Ford said in 1939, "*Think you can…think you can't…you're right either way!*"

Could a Worldwide Epidemic Be Your Defining Moment?

The year was 2003 and the news was filled with the SARS or severe acute respiratory syndrome epidemic. This was also around the same time it seemed there was supposed to be more to life and my career up to that point. I wanted to be able to share the knowledge I gained to date to serve more people. That wasn't going to happen being in a corporate position. What needed to happen for me to become a professional speaker?

Back to the SARS epidemic. It was 2003 and there were 8,000 cases and growing. I wanted to go into the speaking business. I told a friend that ran a seminar company, "If you ever need a speaker, I'm here for you. Any opportunities would be greatly appreciated!"

Suddenly, the SARS epidemic came up and there seemed to be a pretty significant concentration of cases in Toronto. My friend's seminar company was scheduled to do an event in Toronto in August. One day, he gave me a call and asked, "Hey, were you serious about speaking at our events?"

I said, "Absolutely. Why?"

He said, "We had not only one speaker drop out because of the SARS scare, but two." He went on to say, "I'll give you two speaking opportunities and I'll pay you two fees for one event if you'll fill their spots."

My response, "I can either die of SARS or die on stage. Let's do this!" And that became my first paid professional speaking event. Reinvention, here I come!

What was so much fun and so amazing about Toronto was that the headliners for the event included Jack Canfield and Mark Victor Hansen, the co-creators of the *Chicken Soup for the Soul*® series which has sold over 500 million books worldwide.

Jack and Mark were nice enough to come hear me speak, not once, but twice. After the second talk, they walked up to me and Jack said, "Son, what are you doing for a living?" I love remembering the day when Jack Canfield called me son!

I said, "Well, I'm the Vice President of Sales and Marketing for a company in Dallas, but I'm considering going out to speak for a living."

Jack said, "That's a horrible answer! You've been given talents and capabilities most people do not have when it comes to speaking in front of an audience. And if you're not using those talents, you're robbing humanity, you're cheating humanity, and you're being selfish!"

Wow! Not what I was expecting to hear. Both Jack and Mark took the time to take me under their wings and impart some of their genius to me. We've become great friends since then. Jack is one of my mentors and I'm honored to be able to share so much of his wisdom on success.

Mark also took an interest in helping me in my speaking and training career. More than that, Mark was the conduit that helped my heart come to life! Mark invited me to his MEGA Speaking event. This is where I met and started to work with my speaking mentor, John Childers.

And it's also where I met Cynthia Kersey. Cynthia made this impassioned plea to support Habitat for Humanity. At the time, I had no clue what Habitat for Humanity was or what they did. Cynthia delivered her message loud and proud to the audience of around 800 people. She said, "We want women to swing the hammers and drive the nails to build 40 homes in 40 days. Men, the only thing we need you for is your checkbooks!"

I was attending the event with a couple of friends. I turned to my friend on my right side and asked, "Did that hit your heart like it hit mine?"

He said, "I think so. I'm going to write her a $50,000 check!"

I looked at my friend on my left side and he said, "Well, I'm not going to write a $50,000 check, but I am going to write her a $5,000 check."

They both turned towards me and said, "What are you going to do?"

I hung my head and responded, "I can't." I never felt so small in my life.

One friend asked, "What do you mean you can't?"

I said, "I'm in a stock play. We're working to grow this company. I don't have the money to write a check. I can't do that, but I'm committed. I will figure out what to do." I had no idea what that meant at the time. I just knew that I had to do something.

The event ended. I sat in the lobby of the Los Angeles International Airport Marriott getting ready to fly back to Dallas. I thought about all the people I knew. I did know a lot of people with a lot of money. But I couldn't possibly ask my friends for their money to help me, help Cynthia. I had to find a way to make this work. When I told Cynthia that I would somehow find a way to help, I remembered her saying, "Yeah, right." You ever get a, "Yeah, right" before? It kicked me in the gut again, and it was just the motivation I needed.

While I was still sitting there, thinking through what my options might be, I spotted Mark Victor Hansen and Dear Abby walking past me headed toward the restaurant. Mark saw me, too, and said, "Hey Scott, what are you doing? Why don't you come join us for dinner?" I had plenty of time until my scheduled 12:15 a.m. red-eye flight, so I joined them for dinner. Also at dinner, were the remaining speakers from the event, their handlers, and a who's who of amazing people.

It made me think of all the people I have been fortunate enough to meet and get to know. These people were giants in their industries. I've been fortunate enough now, that I've shared the stage with virtually every name you could think of. You might not know my name, but you know theirs.

Sitting there at dinner, it came to me. What if I wrote a book that was about talking to my giant friends? I did just that. And I found out, they haven't always had it easy. They had to persevere in their lives. What I was surprised to find out, was they all had a philanthropic bent. Anybody who has achieved some level of success usually has a natural desire to give back. *Talking with Giants* sprung to life! (Please feel free to download an eBook version at: *http://TWGFreeGift.com*)

Talking with Giants is all about how these individuals achieved what they've achieved. It discusses why they support who they support. *Talking with Giants* (TWG) covers the basic concept that generosity builds prosperity, and not the other way around. You don't prosper and give, rather you give, and then prosper. There are now 21 charities tied to *Talking with Giants*.

Guess what? One of the charities supported by TWG is Habitat for Humanity. The first person I called after Jack agreed to be in, was Cynthia. I called Cynthia and said laughingly, "Okay, troublemaker, you have to be in my book. You are the one that caused this idea to come to life!"

I couldn't write a check, but that didn't mean I couldn't do something to serve the cause. Just because you can't write a check doesn't mean you can't do something. We all have far more connections, know more people, are far more creative than we typically give ourselves credit for. You're perfect just the way you are! Use *your* perfection to accomplish whatever your heart desires. No, I'm not kidding. *You got this!*

Enthusiasm or En Theos – of God's Spirit

One of the key ingredients to living your legacy and creating a life of significance comes through living an enthusiastic lifestyle. Enthusiasm comes from the Greek, *En Theos*, meaning God's Spirit or having God within. Having enthusiasm for all you do and how you do it ultimately makes life more fun, enjoyable, and more worthwhile.

We all go through challenges throughout our lives. Getting through them with grace and dignity, are more times than not, learned behaviors. Seeing the good in all, or at least the learning opportunities, will make your life consistently more pleasant.

Zig Ziglar once said, *"For every sale you miss because you are too enthusiastic, you will miss a hundred because you're not enthusiastic enough."* Waking up each day is a blessing, a miracle, and an opportunity to "make your mark" on all those you interact with throughout the day. What an honor!

My Days in the Prayer Rooms at Get Motivated Seminars

Get Motivated Seminars, originally founded by Peter and Tamara Lowe, were some of the most amazing events I've ever had the honor to present at and be a part of around the country. We had stadiums filled with tens of thousands of people and speaker lineups like no other including former presidents and first ladies, ex-military leaders, business titans, Hall of Fame athletes, former government icons, and many more.

What most people didn't know, is that somewhere in the stadium, was a room full of about 20 to 25 prayer warriors from the neighboring area. These prayer warriors spent the entire day before, during, and after the event praying for the speakers, the audience, the teams, you name it! They prayed for God to give the speakers the wisdom and guidance to present well, make good decisions, and play full-out for the audience to get what they came for from the stellar lineup.

While presenting in front of massive crowds and being part of the buzz was an awesome experience, my time in the prayer rooms is what I truly believed to be the assignment I was to experience during my tenure.

My good friends, Eddie and Alice Smith, ran those prayer rooms. They had a large network of prayer warriors around the country they could call upon. These prayer warriors would selflessly give up a day in their lives to pray and encourage all the speakers, teams, and an arena full of people they would more than likely never meet. These groups were amazing and tremendously powerful.

There are many stories I can share about my times in the prayer rooms. Let me share a few and see if you can observe and learn some of the same things I did through these events.

We were in Austin, Texas and had an extraordinary group of prayer warriors serving our team. That day like at every other event, I visited the prayer room prior to going on stage. We started by having a great conversation, people asking some awesome questions about what it is like to be able to do what I have the honor to do—speak to thousands.

After a while, Eddie and Alice suggested that the group pray over me, one-at-a-time and sometimes multiple people at the same time. It was amazing to have these strangers fill me with so much love, care, and so many blessings.

When everyone finished, I thanked everyone, stood up, and headed out of the room. As I stood up, my now friend, Kenn Renner, stood up and said, "Scott, God just put a verse on my heart for you. Can I share it?"

"Of course, you can", I responded.

Kenn shared, "The verse is Jeremiah 29:11. It says, *"For I know the plans I have for you, declares the Lord. Plans to prosper you, not to harm you. To give you hope and a future!"* Awesome. Does it get any better than that? I went on stage with my encouragement tank filled to the top, gave a great presentation, and had an amazing day.

The very next month we were in Ontario, California. A completely different prayer team, in a completely different state. Prior to my talk, I once again visited the prayer room. We had another great conversation followed by some even more vocal and seemingly powerful prayer over me. As it was time to head off to the stage, a gentleman stopped me and said, "Scott, God just put a verse on my heart for you. Can I share it?"

The way he asked if he could share the message with me, was the same way as the last gentleman. Freaky!

He shared, "It's Jeremiah 29:11. *"For I know the plans I have for you, declares the Lord. Plans to prosper you, not to harm you. To give you hope and a future!"* Now, that's a little wild. Two cities, two different groups, and the exact same verse presented the exact same way. Wow!

Bet you know what's coming next…

A few weeks later, we were at the Thomas and Mack Center in beautiful Las Vegas, Nevada. In what had now become standard operating procedure, I went to visit the prayer room, had another wonderful conversation, with another fabulous group of people. They prayed over me with more amazing prayers. As they finished up their prayers, a female pastor from one of the largest churches in Las Vegas stood up and said… (wait for it…)

"God just put a verse on my heart for you. Can I share it?"

My response was, "Let me prophesy. Jeremiah 29:11 says, *"For I know the plans I have for you, declares the Lord. Plans to prosper you, not to harm you. To give you hope and a future!"*

She said, "How'd you know?"

I share this with you for a number of reasons. The most important of which is God and Jesus Christ, my Higher Source and Creator. Whatever you choose to call your Higher Source, remember that your Higher Source is aspiring for your good. Less than great things happen to good people. It's not the event which ultimately matters. It is the event plus our response to that event that determines our outcomes. Want better outcomes? Learn better responses.

The bottom line is, I'm pretty sure the main reason I had the opportunity to be part of the Get Motivated team was to be able to receive the messages, prayers, and wisdom shared with me in those prayer rooms. The speaking and being able to present to so many incredible audiences was certainly an honor. Sometimes the reason you are in the middle of something is not the reason you think it is at that time. Thank you to *all* the prayer warriors and to Eddie and Alice. You powerfully impacted my life to the positive!

Success Resources and Baptism of the Holy Spirit

Success Resources, another major event company gave me a call in mid-2012. They were about to create a series of events to fill a void that had been left in the market for large stadium-type business seminars. I had been doing more consulting around that time, and they wanted to get me back out on the road and into the fold as one of their regular speakers.

I wasn't sure it was where I was supposed to be at the time. In conversations, the statement made by the promoter was that they believed I was meant to be out on the road with them. After a little more conversation, I agreed to it, as long as I could name the presentation. They wanted me to do, "The Trilogy of Success: Faith, Family, and Focus!" Because I was going to be offering a financial education product at the end, we all agreed that it should then be called, "The Trilogy of Success: Faith, Family, and Finance!"

We were in the Denver Convention Center and the stage was set in the room for 10,000 attendees. I was scheduled to follow Michael J. Fox on stage. It was a tough event. There were technical failures, glitches, and sound bouncing off the concrete floors and walls unmercifully. It was not going well, and the audience was becoming increasingly unsettled.

As it came time for me to pop on stage, I went up and started with the talk. Faith and family were parts of a talk I had given many times. The first 22 minutes of 60 were a breeze. Then we came into the finance portion. In essence, this was what I was really there to present. As I clicked to advance to the next slide, the eight monitors the audience watched and the two monitors on stage for me, all went black!

I had 38 minutes to go, standing on a stage in the round, in the midst of thousands of people, with no monitors, and giving a presentation that had been signed off on by Compliance only three days earlier. To say I didn't have this part of the presentation down pat would be correct.

So, what do you do? You pull from every presentation that was similar to this one over your career and do everything you possibly can to not show that your presentation is down. It's the figurative tap-dance in front of thousands.

The other thing I did was I started having a conversation with God right then and there at the exact same time. Words were coming out of my mouth in semi-auto-pilot mode to the crowd, and my mental thought life was having a full-blown argument with God. HINT: Not a great idea!

Very quickly, I was able to ask why He delivered me this opportunity in the first place—only to totally humiliate me and end my professional speaking career on the spot. I couldn't understand why I was living through this, and yet was able to still give a pretty good presentation even though the screens were down.

I made it through and invited those who wanted to take advantage of the opportunity to go to the tables at the side of the room to register. Immediately upon my mic being shut off, I looked straight up from the middle of the stage and started yelling at God. SECOND HINT: Not a good strategy either!

I looked up, pointing my finger upwards, and said, "God, that is it! I'm done being a hired gun, except for these three things: 1) To share messages of hope and inspiration; 2) To teach and train others to do the same; and 3) To build Your kingdom! Do you hear me?" The crowd was cheering. I think they thought I was still fired up about my talk. I wasn't. I was yelling at God.

As I walked through the crowd to get to the green room, since the stage was in the middle of the convention center floor in the round, people were high fiving me. They shared how powerful the presentation was and thanked me for bringing my faith into the first part of the presentation. It was surreal!

I went to the green room and a woman who spoke earlier in the day, Dr. Clarice Fluitt, said "That was fantastic!"

I unfortunately and rudely responded, "I don't know what you saw, but my professional career is now over!"

She said, "No, you were great!"

I said, "Thank you!" and stormed out of the arena.

I headed straight back to the hotel to change and then go to Jimmy John's for an Unwhich. You see, I only had $7.48 in my pocket. The reason I took this gig in the first place was because of the promise of significant revenue multiple times a month once we went on tour. I was about to be healed of previous financial transgressions. Or, so I thought!

As I came down the elevator to the hotel lobby, the elevator door finally opened. I was walking out the front door of the Denver Downtown Marriott when all of a sudden, I veered left. There at a table in the lobby sat Dr. Clarice Fluitt, her assistant, Tandie, Lance and his wife, Abigale Wallnau. Fellow speaker, Lance had given the gospel message at the event that day.

The next thing I knew, I was approaching their table. When I arrived there, Clarice looked up and invited me to join them. I said, "No, I'm not really in much of a mood. I'm headed to Jimmy John's for an Unwhich. I guess I just came over to you to apologize for being rude when you were so nice to me after I spoke earlier."

Again, Clarice invited me to sit. Again, I said, "No, ma'am!"

She said, "*Sit!*"

I said, "Yes, ma'am!" and I sat.

She said, "Give me your hands and everyone hold hands. Bow your head," and she started praying. Clarice wasn't just praying, she was paarrayying! It was definitely unlike anything I had ever heard or experienced before. When she finished, she said, "Okay, so it's settled. You're joining us for dinner".

"No, ma'am, I'm going to Jimmy John's for an Unwhich."

Clarice said, "No, you'll be joining us. Lance, did you get what I received?" Lance nodded his head, now, they were talking in code.

Clarice looked at me and asked, "Do you know why I asked you to sit and join us?"

Stunned, I responded, "Because you're a nice lady?!"

She smiled and said, "Thank you, I am a nice lady, but that's not it. The reason I asked you to join us is because you were guided to me by an eight-foot angel! You have been assigned to me, and we are going to get to work."

"Excuse me?" I said in pretty much total disbelief. She said that we were going to go to dinner together at The Unsinkable Molly Brown's. And we did. Me and my $7.48 in my pocket and without a single credit card that had any line left on it. Did I say I was going to Jimmy John's for an Unwhich?

Knowing I had no resources to pay for my dinner, I chose the least expense item on the menu and hoped. I hoped that someone was going to offer to take care of the dinner check later.

All throughout dinner, Clarice, Tandie, Lance, and Abigale carried on what seemed to be a fairly interesting conversation. The strangest part of this was that it took place among four people I didn't know. Not only that, these four people all seemed to have insight and knowledge as to who I was and what needed to be done in order to put me on the new and exciting path they knew about, but I didn't.

As we finished dinner, and the check came, it was decided that the check would be split five ways. We would all pay an equal share. Oh no. What now? Well, I pulled out a credit card I knew would not work, at least to save face for that moment.

When the waitress came back, she gave each of us our bills to sign, me included. No, it couldn't be. My card went through. How? There is no way! But it did. That's when Clarice announced, "Okay, so here's the plan. We're going to go back to the hotel. There will be a conference room open. We will go there and set one chair in the middle of the four of us, and we will lay hands on Scott and baptize him in the Holy Spirit." Then she looked at me and said, "I'm sure you don't know exactly what's going on, but you will. And once we're done, hold on. Your life will never be the same!" Boy, was Clarice right on that. September 29, 2012 was definitely a defining moment in my life. Sometimes outside forces will play a part in your reinvention.

It was 10:45 p.m. when we went back to the hotel. Clarice walked up to the front desk to find out which conference room was open and available for an hour or so. Without missing a beat, the front desk agent said, "Chaparral Room, top of the stairs, second floor!" The next thing I knew, they plopped down one chair, had me sit in it, and the four of them surrounded my chair with each of them standing 90 degrees apart.

And that's when it happened. They all laid hands on me and started paaarrraaaying! I don't remember exactly how long it lasted, maybe over an hour. By the time everything concluded, there was no doubt that an intensely spiritual event had just taken place with me being the recipient.

Afterwards, Clarice set out the plan. She said, "Every Tuesday and Wednesday from 10 a.m. to 11 a.m. for the next eight weeks we are going to work together. On Tuesdays, I will impart the teaching, and you are to study and learn. And Wednesdays, you will deliver back to me what you have learned and how you will be putting it into action."

I said, "Dr. Fluitt, I recognize how awesome you are, and how valuable your mentoring will be. How much will you charge for this type of one-on-one attention? While I tremendously appreciate all you have done and are working to do for me, I cannot afford to pay for your mentoring."

That's when she chuckled as only Clarice can and said, "You don't have to worry about that. Your tab has already been picked up by your Father!" Have you ever seen a deer in headlights? I'm pretty sure that's exactly what I must have looked like right then.

Even more stunned than earlier, I asked a simple question, "Why me?"

Clarice said, "Remember when you were on stage yelling at God? Remember when you *declared to Him* that you were done being a hired gun, but rather you were only going to do three things from this point forward? 1) Share messages of hope and inspiration; 2) Teach and train others to do the same; and 3) Build *His* kingdom?"

"Yes, of course", I responded.

She said, "*He* heard you. *He* believed you and *He* will never let you out of it. Hold on. Your life will never be the same!"

I'm sure at this point, there are a number of readers in varying stages of belief or even disbelief. As I wrote this account, I shared with a great friend, Sean G. Murphy, that I wasn't sure how much of this I was going to include. Then, I realized that this wasn't really my work anyway.

Part of sharing my story is to help others gain the courage to share their own experiences, so they can move on with their mission. I want to lift these people up to acknowledge they are not the only ones who've had this type of experience. I encourage you, if this includes you, to journal your experience, and relive it as you write it down. I truly believe you will finally find the clarity you may be looking for, from your experiences.

His Plan and Timing Are Perfect!

We will dive deep into how His plan and timing are perfect as well as many other spiritual topics throughout this work. Before doing so, if it has not been obvious, let me clear up any confusion. I am a believer in God and Jesus Christ.

And as such, it is not my place to make you believe what I believe. It is my place to be a living example of my belief, be representative of my belief, and encourage you to have a belief in whatever you choose as your higher source. My Christian belief is another topic we will dive into further as this work proceeds.

So How Do You Get on the Right Track?

Again, my encouragement to you would be to start by determining your foundational makeup. A few of my friends had shared a similar encouragement with me in wanting to make sure I had a strong place to start. Let's try this exercise. Write down a list of values you cherish in life. Then, identify the top five or six that most resonate with who you are. Sometimes asking a close friend or confidant can be an advantage to help you understand who you really are and what you stand for. As the old axiom says, "If you don't stand for something, you'll fall for anything!" Here are my core values:

Core Values – Five Founding Principles

Faith is belief in a higher source. It is trusting in a higher source's plan and timing for all the events in your life. Having faith is living a life full of the fruit of the spirit: love, joy, peace, patience, kindness, goodness, faithfulness, gentleness, and self-control.

Honesty refers to a facet of moral character and denotes positive and virtuous attributes such as integrity, truthfulness, and straight forwardness along with the absence of lying, cheating, and theft.

Integrity is a concept of consistency of actions, values, methods, measures, principles, expectations, and outcomes. In ethics, integrity is regarded as the honesty, truthfulness, or accuracy of one's actions.

Courage is having the quality of mind and spirit to address things head-on and a willingness to face fear and push through adversity, rather than run from it.

Stewardship is an ethic that embodies responsible planning and management of resources. The concept of stewardship has been applied in diverse realms, including with respect to the environment, economics, health, property, information, and religion. It is linked to the concept of sustainability.

Answers for When It's Not Only About You...
but for Those Who Count on You!

Where Do We Go from Here?

My encouragement for you now is to review this work critically, pick out the things you like, and challenge the things that don't rest as easily for you. Think them through, put them into practice, try new things on, see what fits and what doesn't at the moment.

Use this material as a resource for you to "dial-it-in" to your best life possible. As you venture through this process, you may find yourself sharing tidbits with those you love or even those who happen to cross your path. Who knows who you might influence along the way? We're all on this journey together. Personally, I'm looking forward to making the rest of my life the best of my life. How about you?

What Do You Do When Your Car Attacks You?

When it comes to my car accident, people often ask when this happened and how? Let me share another one of my life-changing events with you.

I was going to a speaking event on December 6th, 2014. As I went out to load a box of books into my SUV, I made it to my car, then balanced the box on one knee. As I was balancing that box, I threw the back hatch skyward so fast I ducked underneath it. As quickly as I lifted it up, it flew back down and hit me on the back of my head. This nearly cold-cocked me. You know, like in the cartoons, where the stars are circling around the character's head? It was like that. I mean, I was woozy.

Four days later, I had to fly out to California to take part in an infomercial shoot. I boarded the plane and as we reached altitude, it felt like my head was going to blow off. Even my traveling companion noticed saying, "It's not like you to put down your book and not read while we're flying." I just couldn't focus. Something wasn't right.

Later that day, we finished up the infomercial shoot in Los Angeles. And afterwards, I decided to attend Angelus Temple and the Dream Center. As you can recall from earlier on in this book (page 49), this is when I proceeded to have a stroke. While heading to University City Walk for lunch, I completely lost the ability to move my legs.

I was rushed to the emergency room and remained there for five hours. The medical staff seemed to have done every test known to man and womankind. Nobody could figure out exactly what was going on with me.

A couple of my buddies, Mitch Edland and Mike Escobedo, stayed with me and were part of the group praying over me throughout my time in the emergency room. It would be 30 days later when we would see each other again, to have lunch, and reconstruct everything that went on that day. I am tremendously grateful to Mitch and Mike and the rest of our travel party for their support during this time!

After hours in the emergency room, they finally released me with a "major migraine" and suggested I get back to my hotel and try to get some rest. Yeah, right! How could I rest with Lynard Skynard and the entire cast of that season of *Survivor* in the lobby of our hotel? They were there to film the finale. Too bad so sad for me!

As I went up to my room. My head felt like it was about to blow off. The pain was unbearable. It actually became so bad I had to cry out, "God, help!"

This is the only time in my life I heard an audible voice from God saying, "Drop to your knees!"

I slid out of bed and I dropped to my knees. I had my elbows up on the bed and I said, "Lord, for the last couple of years, I have been teaching that your plan and your timing are perfect. I do not pretend to understand this plan or this timing. I do not believe your plan is to call me home. I do not believe your plan is to maim me or disable me. So, I'm choosing to believe your plan is to wake me up. Duly noted, you have my attention! I believe I'm supposed to use this event to save myself and serve others physically and spiritually for the rest of my life.

And if that is your will for my life, I ask for your wisdom and guidance going forward, so I can implement your plan appropriately. And if that's not your will for my life, I just want you to know, whatever you have planned for me, I'm good with it!"

I went to climb into bed, but instead, I felt like I climbed onto a cloud, in total peace, zero pain, and fell straight to sleep. I woke up the next morning, showered, dressed, and went on set. I shot three television shows. These took 53 minutes, 18 minutes, and 14 minutes. Before the cameras went live, I was sitting slumped over in a chair when the producer whispered into my ear. He'd come over to say, "You know, when we go live, we're going to need you."

I said, "Don't worry about me. I'll be just fine."

They'd get me up on set and then say, "Five, four, three, two, one!" As soon as it was time to talk, I was ready to go. In between takes, I retreated to my chair off stage to fold up like a wet blanket.

That afternoon, after the shooting wrapped, I went to a neurologist for another examination because the pain was still pretty intense. He said, "I think you have trapped occipital nerves radiating these headaches. We need an MRI, but we can't get that done until tomorrow."

The next day, 48 hours after the initial event, I completed the MRI. After reading the results of the MRI, the neurologist's first words to me were, "Get your ass to the hospital and check into the ICU. You've had a stroke!" It was then that I was virtually scared to death. I felt like a breakable China doll and spent the next six days in intensive care.

My time in the ICU was unique to say the least. I'm pretty sure they weren't preoccupied trying to keep me alive. It seemed far more as if they were trying to understand why I was *still* alive. At one point, I heard the doctors talking to the entire team. The neurologist said he had done the angiogram. They inserted a metal probe into my brain and verified what they had thought happened. At the turn in the PICA or posterior interior cerebellar artery, there was a dissection—a separation of the inner and outer walls of the artery interfering with blood flow.

They kept saying, "We have no clue how this could be the way it is, and he's still okay. We don't understand it."

Since I could hear the doctor talking, I said, "Hey Doc, I have it all figured out!"

The neurosurgeon leaned into my room and asked, "What?"

I told him I had it all figured out.

He replied, "Okay." The whole team came into my room and the doctor continued, "Okay, smart ass. What is it?"

I said, "Well, it's obvious. It's God's grace, mercy, and favor on my life!"

He then said, "Well, that's as good an answer as we have!" And they all walked out.

There are so many more stories and hilarious anecdotes surrounding my stay at the hospital. They could fill an entire chapter. To stay on point, we'll save them for another day.

My stroke happened mid-afternoon on Sunday, December 14th, 2014. After being released from the emergency room, spending six days in the ICU, and two days on set, I wasn't allowed to get on an airplane to fly back to Dallas, until January 2nd.

Finally, arriving back in Dallas, I was working to normalize my life and get back into the swing of things. One of the first events I attended outside my house was Celebration Saturday—ID Life Corporate on Saturday, January 10th. It was great to be back and mingling with so many friends and well-wishers.

A friend of mine, Darlene Unclebach, came up to chat with me that day. She asked if I had any residual effects from anything I had been through just weeks earlier.

I said, "It's really weird. I have a little tingling on the tips of four fingers on my left hand. They kind of feel like they are at 90 percent capacity to feel." I went on to say, "Every once in a while, I get this pressure just above my wrist on my left forearm. It's like someone is grabbing me, squeezing hard for a minute, and then releasing it."

Darlene asked, "When do you feel that?"

I said, "When I'm working through a decision, like, how am I going to move forward from this? How am I going to get going and get back to work?"

She started laughing. Don't you hate it when someone has information that you don't have? And you're curious to know what it is? I inquired, "What are you laughing about?"

She then said, "You don't get what that is? It happens every time you go to make a decision about your future for yourself."

I said, "Yeah, go on."

She replied, "It's pretty obvious to me that it's God grabbing you and saying, *I have this! I have you!*"

Darlene suggested I *sit on a rock* for 30 days and not make any decisions about my future. Interestingly enough, as I stopped working so hard to get back in the game, that feeling of being grabbed and held, disappeared.

Plano Chamber of Commerce — Women's Division

Prior to my stroke, I was scheduled to speak at the Plano Chamber's Women's Division Luncheon. As the date arrived, I was feeling great, heck it was a full 30 days since my stroke. I committed to the event, so of course you go present and fulfill your commitment!

I was teaching the women how to sell more in their businesses. The whole room was full of women. Somewhere along my presentation, I said, "Business can be tough. Sometimes you just have to persevere. Heck, 30 days ago, I had a full-blown cerebellar stroke!" I kind of just dropped this bombshell into my talk and continued on presenting.

Afterwards, I was signing books and a woman came up to me and said, "Did you say that 30 days ago you had a full-blown cerebellar stroke?"

I replied, "Yes, I did."

She said, "People don't come out like you."

So, I said, "If you say so! This is the only experience I've ever had. Why do you say that?"

She then said, "Because I'm with the American Heart and Stroke Association."

"Good, then use me." I told her.

She then replied, "We can't pay you."

And I said, "I never asked to be paid. I asked to be used. If my story is so unique, why don't you use me to help share your message!" What do they say you do when you have lemons? Make lemonade! In the first three galas that were put together for the American Heart and Stroke Association, we raised over $750,000.

God has been great. We've raised close to one million dollars for heart and stroke research. Do you understand that no matter what's going on in your life, and I am not minimizing anything that's happened in your life by any stretch of the imagination, God's plan and timing are perfect?

You can't say I shouldn't have had a stroke and become upset about this negative event. If God's plan and timing are perfect, it usually means being excited about a positive event or outcome. You can say one or the other, but you can't believe they are both true! I choose to believe that God's plan and timing are perfect.

There's a pretty good book out there that says, "*as we know,*" all things work for the good of those who believe and are called to His purpose. While we may not understand why we are going through what we are going through, that event has been put into our lives for our benefit. Trust it will benefit you! If not now, eventually! If not for you, for someone else!

All things, not some things. All things are for your good.

Chapter 5

LIVE DON'T LEAVE YOUR LEGACY

Seven Steps to Living Your Legacy

As I worked to build a regular routine again, I realized that living through a near-death experience changed the way you thought about virtually everything in your life. I know this probably seems like a no-brainer and that it should be a given. But I also realized that I never read a book about what you do when you're still alive.

I remember one of the first things I looked up after getting out of the ICU was, "How long do stroke victims wait to drive again?" Trust me, the answer was a total shock! It said that because of the severity of injury of most strokes of the brain, most patients *never* drive again. What? Are you kidding me? I certainly didn't like that answer, so I looked up something else.

"How long do stroke victims wait to speak again?" I wanted to check the recommended time for a professional speaker to regain their strength, balance, etc., so I could start planning to be back on stage. The answer was that many stroke patients *never* regain the ability to speak and therefore never resume their careers. What the…?

I was more shaken by what I was reading and learning after the fact, than what I had already lived through. It was crazy! I finally decided that if anyone was going to help people who had experienced anything close to what I had experienced, it would probably have to be me.

That's when I started thinking deeper about things. The concepts about legacy became far more important. As did Significance versus Success. When you live through something like this, your thought process changes a bunch!

Because I had some time on my hands while I recovered, I did some deeper study into legacy, and what it truly meant to strive for significance in your life. Some think significance is only a status thing. I, in turn, would rather look at the entire definition. Significance is the meaning behind the accomplishment. Life and legacy had become all about meaning.

That's when I developed *The Seven Steps to Living Your Legacy*. This developed around six areas of life, plus legacy. As it started to come together, so did the acronym to tie this work around one major theme— B.A.L.A.N.C.E. Living your legacy is really about understanding and achieving the ever illusive B.A.L.A.N.C.E. in our lives.

The Seven Steps to Living Your Legacy are achieved by living life in B.A.L.A.N.C.E. This would include our spiritual, professional, physical, financial, social, and personal areas of our lives, plus our legacy. Over the next few chapters, you'll learn just how important all of this is to live a fulfilled, happy, productive, and rewarding life!

B.A.L.A.N.C.E.

Let's go ahead and address the elephant in the room immediately. There *is no* such thing as work-life balance. It is a myth, unless of course you can divide yourself into seven directions at any one time.

The true concept to achieve balance is actually what I call *purposeful imbalance* or more appropriately, *presence*! If you truly want to accomplish the most possible in any given time frame, it comes through undivided attention and focus in that particular moment. *Be* present doing what you are doing!

If you want to play full-out in life, my encouragement to you would be to learn to become tremendously present. *Be where your feet are!* We live in a very self-centered society. Many people you encounter daily have the attention span of a gnat. Sorry, I'm not working to demean gnats!

With so much clamoring for our attention, those who have refined the skill of being totally present in any situation are finding great success. Their success happens in the exact same encounter with someone else, whose focus is split by their mobile phone or another sensory overload device.

In order to truly achieve overall balance, you must be absolutely focused on one thing during a defined time frame. Too many people are attempting to multi-task, which is just another word for doing many things poorly at the same time! The picture below hopefully gives you a visual depiction of this concept.

Let the concentric circles represent one through ten, with one being in the middle, disengaged, and the outer ring ten, playing full-out. Let's examine the plotting. Spiritually you're at a four, professionally at an eight, physically at a three, financially at a three, socially at a *12*, your legacy contribution at about 1.5, and personally at a five. The reality is, if ten is optimal, you aren't really playing full-out, except for maybe a little bit too much socially.

How do you fix this? It's actually pretty simple. Whenever you are in any particular category, *be* fully present. If you're at work, *be* a ten! If you're at church, *be* a ten! If you're volunteering, *be* up at ten! Whatever your area of concentration at that time, *be* there fully!

I heard a fabulous speaker sharing a story one day. He said, a little boy came up to his dad while he was watching a football game on television. The little boy started talking to his dad and finally asked him, "Daddy, are you listening to me?"

The father replied, "Of course, I am."

To which the little boy said, "Daddy, listen with your eyes!" The little boy was asking, in his own way, for his father to look him square in the eyes while they were talking. *Be* present! If that doesn't make the point, I'm not sure what would.

Another quick thought for your consideration. Have you ever noticed that the words *listen* and *silent* contain the exact same letters, but in a different order? Is it possible that the very best way for any of us to listen is to remain silent? The good Lord was on our side when we were created. We've been given two ears and one mouth. I'm pretty sure that means we are supposed to listen twice as much as we speak! Truly take in the words being shared with you, and then and only then, respond accordingly.

Give an increased level of presence in every conversation and interaction. It won't take long to grasp how much better you can be, when you play full-out and make every interaction a ten.

Yesterday is history.

Tomorrow is a mystery.

Today is a gift.

That's why today is called – the present!

Believe in a Higher Source

The B in B.A.L.A.N.C.E. stands for Believe in a Higher Source.

This is your spiritual foundation. For me, that's God and Jesus Christ. For you, it might be Buddha, Allah, Shiva, or the Universe. Whatever you choose to call your higher source is fine with me. My God says to be a living example of your beliefs, and to leave the heavy lifting and the conversions to Him.

Be someone that somebody wants to follow because of what they observe from your actions. The fact of the matter is, out of the 137 times Jesus spoke to people in the marketplace, 122 of those times he basically said, "Follow me!" That's the command, to follow. *Be* a living example of your beliefs.

Again, I am not working to put my beliefs upon you. What I am suggesting is you need to believe in something. If you think you are the highest power on earth, you're not. If you think you are all-knowing on this planet, there's a lot of pressure on you. That means everything that happens anywhere on earth, is on you.

Personally, I don't want all that responsibility. What I want to do is to be able to take and share what I'm living through with my Higher Source, who can guide and comfort me along the way. Again, I'm not trying to get you to believe what I believe, but I'm encouraging you to believe in something, whatever that may be. By the way, I'm certainly happy to talk with you about this if it helps you!

How did I learn this lesson? Here's another story to share how I experienced my Higher Source. A few professional speakers and I went to Singapore for an event. It wasn't until after the event that I found out that only ten percent of the country was Christian. I was about to go on stage. There were about 5,000 people out in the audience, and we were doing a speaker panel. There were seven of the speakers, from throughout the day, sitting in chairs ready to field questions from T. Harv Eker, the event host.

Each speaker was asked a question and given a chance to answer before it was the next speaker's turn. The microphone was passed to the person in the next chair as each answer was shared. We each had about a minute to a minute and a half to answer the question. After the seven of us finished answering the first question, the microphone came back up the line for the next question. I was in the third chair and we had already gone down to the last person and come back around again the second time. We were now on the third question.

The third question was, "What's your highest value?"

Keith Cunningham sat in chair number one and said, "Well, for everything that's been happening in my life, it has to be integrity." Keith went on to give the best answer on integrity in the history of all mankind. It was awesome. The only problem was, I was now thinking,

Crud, integrity was my answer!

Keith passed the microphone to Saen Higgins, sitting in the second chair. Saen looks at Keith and says, "Thanks, that was my answer!" Well, no one could beat Keith's answer on integrity, so I decide I'm going to say courage. Saen then went on to give an equally excellent answer about courage. It was the best answer on courage you ever heard in your life.

Crud, that was my second answer!

Saen goes to hand me the mic, and I have nothing. I mean zero. They just gave the best answers imaginable for integrity and now, courage. I have nothin'! So, I did what any good speaker would do. I started stalling with the ole' pregnant pause.

Remember, my pre-stage prayer was, "Lord, allow my words to impact 100 percent of the lives in this audience positively in one way, shape, or form. Only You know who You sent to hear this message. Allow me to do the best I can to deliver that message. Let me be a vehicle and of service to You." I had given *Him* permission to take me over. *He* took me over!

Saen handed me the mic. I grabbed the mic with nothing, stood up slowly, and dramatically, and I said, "Well, it's belief in a higher source. For me, that's God and Jesus Christ. For you, it might be Buddha, Allah,

Hinduism, the Universe, whatever you choose to call it I'm fine with. If you think you're the highest being on this planet, you're making a mistake, because you're not it. You have to have faith. You have to have faith in something higher than yourself. My God says to be a living example of your beliefs. Let Him do the heavy lifting and the conversion. However, if you don't have faith, you have nothing in your life!"

I handed the microphone to the next person in line and sat down. I looked up and started laughing. I had never said those words in my life. I sat there for that period of time looking up and started having a conversation with God. "Really, *You* choose *now* to take me over? Seriously?"

I continue having a conversation with God, while the guy next to me is answering the same question to the audience. We end up there for another hour to an hour and a half answering several more questions. Through the rest of our time on stage, I'm sitting there not thinking too much about anything else except, wow, this is a pretty wild experience.

As I come off stage, there are four Muslim women in full regalia at the bottom of the stairs. They said, "Mr. Scott, can we get our picture with you?"

I said, "I'd be honored. Wait a second. Please hear and understand my heart. I don't presume to understand your culture, but I didn't think you did a lot of picture-taking."

"Oh, we don't. We only take pictures of people or things we want to honor."

"Well, that's very nice. Why would you want to honor me?"

"Because you made us cry," one of the Muslim ladies replied.

"Okay, now I'm confused. You want to honor me, because I made you cry? Help me understand this."

They said, "Mr. Scott, for the first time in our lives, you encouraged us to have faith. You didn't try to convert us. For that, we honor you."

I've told this story from the stage many times. What if those four Muslim women were married to the worst terrorists in Southeast Asia? What if, because of this one interaction, they finally met one Westerner, one Christian, and realized we're not so bad? What if, because of this, some heinous act was either lessened or not done at all? I have no way to prove any what-ifs and no way to disprove them. What if we were all just the living examples we've been asked to be? What if? What could we do in this world?

Do you understand this is the power that each and every one of you hold? I'm just one guy, but this has been put on my heart to share with you to start the ripple effect. The reason this needs to be a book is so that you can share this concept, to experience and continue the ripple effect for yourself.

Do you understand there's one definition that exists which defines two different words? That definition is *confidence in the unseen and assurance of the unknown*. This definition defines two words: fear and faith. Fear is confidence in the unseen and assurance of the unknown. Fear is a belief in something negative. Faith is confidence in the unseen and assurance of the unknown. Faith is belief in something positive.

Here's the point to ponder. There is only one place on the planet where this definition is assigned, and it happens to be in the Bible. In Hebrews 11:1 it says, *"Faith is confidence in the unseen, assurance of the unknown."* You have the choice to side with either fear or faith. What are you going to believe?

In a business, if you don't have faith, you don't have a business, because there is no assurance that anybody will ever come through your doors. There is no assurance that anybody will ever buy your products. There is no assurance that anybody will ever work with you. Yet, you're being entrepreneurial and have a business.

Whether you want to admit it or not, by default, the fact that you have a business demonstrates that you have faith. As long as you already have faith, my encouragement to you is to embrace it.

Faith itself has three parts. The first is knowledge of your belief. It's the ask. The second is agreement with your belief. That's the believe. And the third is trust in your belief. That is the receive! *Ask, believe, and receive.* The more you embrace your belief, the deeper you will understand that God's plan and timing are perfect!

I used to teach that God's plan and timing are perfect, but that it's rare to understand it. I don't teach it this way anymore. Today, I teach that God's plan and timing are perfect, and I'm going to suggest you can never understand it! Trust and rest in the fact that God is aspiring to do great things in your life. I've found that when I rest in this concept, tremendous peace comes over me.

What have I done to help verify and validate that God's plan and timing are perfect in my life? I created an *Evidence Log.* When things, which I have prayed for, even random things, happen throughout my life, I write them down in my Evidence Log. They are evidence of God's goodness and *His* delivering on *His* promises. *He* is a just-in-time God. And also, an always-when-you-need *Him* God.

Keeping this Evidence Log allows me to go back and review all the good that happened, even when everything may not seem so great. It also gives me the encouragement to truly *be* a living example of my beliefs. Easily one of the best and easiest ways to *be* a living example is to treat *all people with dignity, honor, and respect.*

All of us have been wonderfully made in the image of our Creator. Recognize this fact, lift others up, and provide them the dignity they are due. Honor who they are and what they are working to do to contribute to mankind. Respect their choices on how they add to the greater good. *Be* an encourager. It really doesn't take that much effort or even cost a lot of money to encourage people. It's amazing how something as little as a smile can and does make a positive difference in so many people's lives!

We all have the opportunity to share in the fruit of the Spirit. As I have been studying to complete this work, I came across the following details about how we can use and share this fruit in our lives, as shown by Scott Williams.

But the fruit of the Spirit is love, joy, peace, patience, kindness, goodness, faithfulness, gentleness, self-control. (Galatians 5:22-23)

Each of these is a characteristic of the Holy Spirit's active presence in our daily activities. Let's look at each one and ask some diagnostic questions to make sure we're healthy.

Love. *This word for love doesn't refer to warm feelings but to a deliberate attitude of good will and devotion to others. Love gives freely without looking at whether the other person deserves it, and it gives without expecting anything back.*

Question: Am I motivated to do for others as Christ has done for me, or am I giving in order to receive something in return?

Joy. *Unlike happiness, joy is gladness that is completely independent of the good or bad things that happen in the course of the day. In fact, joy denotes a supernatural gladness given by God's Spirit that actually seems to show up best during hard times. This is a product of fixing your focus on God's purposes for the events in your life rather than on the circumstances.*

Question: Am I experiencing the joy of life on a regular basis, or is my happiness dependent on things going smoothly in my day?

Peace. *It's not the absence of turmoil, but the presence of tranquility even while in a place of chaos. It is a sense of wholeness and completeness that is content knowing that God controls the events of the day.*

Question: Do I find myself frazzled by the crashing waves of turmoil in my life, or am I experiencing "the peace that passes all comprehension" (Philippians 4:6-7)?

Patience. *Other words that describe this fruit are lenience, long-suffering, forbearance, perseverance, and steadfastness. It is the ability to endure ill treatment from life or at the hands of others without lashing out or paying back.*

Question: Am I easily set off when things go wrong or people irritate me, or am I able to keep a godly perspective in the face of life's irritations?

Kindness. When kindness is at work in a person's life, he or she looks for ways to adapt to meet the needs of others. It is moral goodness that overflows. It's also the absence of malice.

Question: Is it my goal to serve others with kindness, or am I too focused on my own needs, desires, or problems to let the goodness of God overflow to others?

Goodness. While kindness is the soft side of good, goodness reflects the character of God. Goodness in you desires to see goodness in others and is not beyond confronting or even rebuking—as Jesus did with the money changers in the temple—for that to happen.

Question: Does my life reflect the holiness of God, and do I desire to see others experience God at a deep level in their own lives?

Faithfulness. A faithful person is one with real integrity. He or she is someone others can look to as an example, and someone who is truly devoted to others and to Christ. Our natural self always wants to be in charge, but Spirit-controlled faithfulness is evident in the life of a person who seeks good for others and glory for God.

Question: Are there areas of hypocrisy and indifference toward others in my life, or is my life characterized by faith in Christ and faithfulness to those around me?

Gentleness. Meekness is not weakness. Gentleness is not without power; it just chooses to defer to others. It forgives others, corrects with kindness, and lives in tranquility.

Question: Do I come across to others as brash and headstrong, or am I allowing the grace of God to flow through me to others?

Self-control. Our fleshly desires, Scripture tells us, are continually at odds with God's Spirit and always want to be in charge. Self-control is literally releasing our grip on the fleshly desires, choosing instead to be controlled by the Holy Spirit. It is power focused in the right place.

Question: Are my fleshly desires controlling my life, or am I allowing the Spirit to direct me to the things that please God and serve others?

Walk by the Spirit. *While not a fruit of the Spirit, the final item on the checkup produces all nine qualities listed above. When we follow the Spirit's lead instead of being led by our self-focused desires, He produces the fruit.*

But even when we don't walk by the Spirit, He is the very one who convicts us that things are not in proper order in our lives.

God promises that if we are willing to admit that we have been walking our own way and ask for His forgiveness and cleansing, He will empower us through His Spirit to live above ourselves and live the abundant life for which He has created us.

Question: Am I actively depending on the Holy Spirit to guide me in God's ways, so I don't get wrapped up in myself? If not, am I willing to confess to God that His ways are better than mine, and that I need the Spirit's guidance to live above the fray?

Thank you, Scott Williams, for your reflection on the fruit of the Spirit and allowing us all to benefit from such a greater understanding.

Morning Quiet Time

To solidify my beliefs, and to practice reaching up and hearing from God, I have designated a quiet time for myself each morning. Many times, I read the Bible. Sometimes, I sit with the material from Bob Beaudine's book, *2 Chairs*. Bob shares an amazing process that always provides benefits. My encouragement to you is to get his book, *2 Chairs*, and put the process and steps Bob shares to action in your life.

More often than not, my morning routine includes going into the steam room at the Las Colinas Sports Club. It is there that I pray the Lord's Prayer, extend gratitude for everything happening in my life at that time, and ask the questions, "Lord, what would you have me do today?" or "Who would you have me reach out to today?" These questions typically spur me on to activities later on in the day.

Then I sit, sweat, and wait to see what shows up in my awareness. Hopefully, it comes in a fairly timely manner. Did I say I was in a steam room? Invariably, something shows up!

One day, it was to call a certain person who I hadn't talked to in at least seven months. When I called later that morning, he shared a new project he was involved in. Then, he asked me if I wanted to participate in it as well. Interesting, huh?

Personally, I don't slow down all that well. People who know me recognize that I am an incredible action-taker and tend to work off the sequence Ready–Fire–Aim (Tom Peters) which is pretty much my process. I'm a huge believer that the only way to gain feedback is to have some type of movement preceding it. I realize I don't always make the right decisions or take the right actions. I have, however, become pretty good at making course corrections quicker and more often than most. I pray daily to understand and implement things better and faster.

My morning quiet times are an example of something I have added to my life. It helps me consistently work to improve things. These quiet times allow me to slow down long enough to gain some guidance from my Higher Source, so that I can do the work *He* has designed for me long ago. Incorporate a little listening time in your day. I am pretty sure you will be amazed at what and who starts to show up!

Align Yourself Professionally

The A in B.A.L.A.N.C.E. stands for Align Yourself Professionally.

This is in regard to your career and professional area. The bottom line is, you have to be purposeful and live with intention and passion. Do you think I'm passionate about what I do? I *know* that this is what I'm supposed to do professionally. I know that I'm here to serve you and to share the knowledge that I've gained over my career. This is to help you grow and to help you become ready, so you can help others grow, too.

We have the opportunity to start the ripple by being a new rock thrown in the pond. Then, we let the ripples grow and encourage those ripples to go further. The only way you're going to be able to do that with whatever it is you do, is to give it everything you have. As Jack Canfield says in the book, *The Success Principles*™, 100 percent is easy, 99 percent is a bitch. And that's a fact!

Are you all-in or are you not all-in? If you're all-in, this is the one place to be. Personally, I am all-in for serving my call. This is not about a product. It's about the call of growing people. This is my call. I can utilize products, systems, or education, but you understand, it's really about understanding the call. It's understanding what your God-given talents and capabilities allow you to do.

My life's purpose statement is to *inspire and empower others to serve humanity through living their life's purpose in spirit, love, and joy!* Do you recognize that while I'm writing this material, just sharing it with you puts me *on purpose*? It feels awesome. I was asked yesterday how I keep my energy level up. I told this person that it was easy. I get to give. I get to be enthused. I get to be in spirit and be enthusiastic. All this only increases my energy.

Dr. John Demartini, a good friend, and one of the teachers in *The Secret*, is just an amazing international thought leader. At a time when I did 288 talks that year, he was doing 320. I thought I did a lot. I asked, "John, don't you ever get tired?"

He said, "Tired? How can you get tired doing what you've been called to do, and you love to do?"

I encourage you in whatever your pursuit is, to find the one thing that makes your heart leap. The one thing that just inspires you completely. The thing you will fight through anything for to get the opportunity to do. Recently, I spoke at three chiropractic colleges. Chiropractors are wonderful people working to bring a holistic health message to the world, and yet they are maligned. They are shot at, not literally, but figuratively. They are called names. And these are people committed to serving the greater good.

I shared this with them, "You have to know that you know that you know that you know that the only thing that heals the body is the body. When you align the spine, you allow the divine to do its work. You need to be able to share that message with people, so that we can all understand that the only thing that heals the body is the body. You have to have the passion behind it. You have to have the purpose behind it."

"If we could get everybody to understand that the only thing that heals the body is the body, we wouldn't have a problem with insurance, because they would pay for chiropractic care, because anything that allows the body to heal, they pay for. You wouldn't take drugs, because the only thing that heals the body is the body. For the most part, the drug only masks the symptoms."

With my stroke situation, I went from zero prescriptions to seven. I can tell you that in 90 days, one of the prescriptions started to turn me into a blithering idiot. This is a medication the vast majority of the CEOs in this country are on. And we wonder why we're going downhill. Somebody is probably saying, "Oh, don't worry about the facts. This happens to be just a cholesterol medicine. It's not that common, right?"

Major side effects from this prescription include balance issues and memory loss. I'm a professional speaker. Let's take a look at the area of balance. Let's see. To speak, I stand up all the time. But what are the consequences if I have balance issues? Or memory loss, for that matter? C-Suites around the world, including myself, are accepting these prescriptions and their side effects, because somebody says we should. The body is designed to be perfect. If it's not perfect, it's something we did whether it's emotional, chemical, or physical stress. Change this. Stop it. It's your choice. We can do it together.

If you want to be a leader, *be* lead-worthy! And also, know that at some point, every great leader was an excellent follower. Leaders share their core values and make sure their team knows their vision and mission. You have to have guidelines and goals to lead a team to the finish line. Casting vision is important, too. "Where there is no vision, the people perish!"

Being and staying on purpose is much easier when you have a life purpose statement. It becomes the filter by which future decisions are tested and evaluated. Writing this material? Let's do a test: To inspire and empower others to live their purpose? Yes, that's all who are reading this book. Am I living my purpose in the Spirit? I'm aligned and closer to God than I have ever been. Love? I love my wife, my family, and my friends more than I ever have. Joy? Producing this work, which you are absorbing brings me joy!

It is important to have a life purpose statement to guide you in making better and more quality decisions on a daily basis. Clearly knowing what you stand for makes it far easier to develop a group or company vision. It is important to be congruent in your actions, words, and deeds.

Then, you take your purpose and you fuel it with passion. My career is about sending messages that serve you, the audience. It is invigorating! Are you committed enough to serve and save some people on this planet? That becomes the question. If you don't have the passion behind what you're doing, nobody is going to join you. You won't take the lead if you are not passionate about the project.

Here's one more thought to ponder. Long ago, I created a quote that ties directly to the professional area. It is, when you have a big enough what, and a strong enough why, the how shows up! Let me break it down for you. When you have a big enough *what* you want to accomplish in your life, a strong enough *why* you want to do it, then the *how to* accomplish it shows up.

Far too often, people go around asking the wrong questions professionally. *How* am I going to accomplish whatever it is that I want to accomplish? It truly is the wrong question. When you know *what* you want to do and *why* you want to do it, the *how* to do it shows up!

I had been a national sales trainer and sales guy forever. However, my heart was telling me that I wanted to, and had the ability to reach more people. Initially, I didn't know how that was going to happen. Resting fully into the desire of serving more people and believing in the fact that God had granted me a solid skill set, it became evident that I could accomplish my desires by becoming a professional speaker and trainer.

Find the profession, the job, and the way to generate income that turns your vocation into a vacation. *I love speaking! I love training! I love coaching* and helping others achieve their dreams and desires! What is going to get your heart to leap, so you can have the career of your dreams?

Live a Healthy Lifestyle

The L in B.A.L.A.N.C.E. stands for Live a Healthy Lifestyle.

This is your physical being. In many of my presentations, as we come to this physical piece, I ask the audience the question, "How many of you are planning to stay in your body for the rest of your life?" Most people raise their hands.

The fact of the matter is, you only have one body. Let that sink in. If you trash it, you're done. You can have all the money in the world and if you don't have your health, the only thing you're left wanting is your health. Without your health, nothing else is possible.

Hear my heart. I write this as an absolute reminder for me as well as for you. I was 27 pounds at six months old, 41 pounds as a one-year-old, and 92 pounds in the first grade. I have lived what it is like to have your weight fluctuate in some pretty big swings. There is zero judgement toward you on my part, only empathy.

If you are not the size and weight you want to be, the good news is that there is something that can be done about it. Permanent improvement is possible and even likely should you make the decision to do what it takes to maximize your health.

Why Improve Your Lifestyle?

I believe each individual has been born into greatness and is entitled to live the life of their dreams. That means living a life by choice, not chance. It's being able to fully experience all life has to offer.

Individually, you have been designed to live your purpose and passion by living life to its fullest—not trudging through each day.

So, what's your most valuable asset? When asked, most people respond with, "My health!" How true! It's worth repeating that without your health, nothing else in life is possible.

Beyond your health, most people want to love and be loved. They want to share significant time and moments with others they care about, and make a difference. All that and more is available when you make decisions and take actions to improve your lifestyle.

Where do you want to live? Where would you travel to if money was no object? What college would you send your kids to? What cause or causes would you support? Who would you like to meet? Who would you like to have as your mentor? What is on your bucket list?

When you control your lifestyle and your future, you get to create both the questions and answers to your life!

Why is This So Important?

Unfortunately, in this day and age when so much help is available, Americans are dying off or succumbing to disease at alarming rates due to unhealthy lifestyles. Again, no judgement, just want to share this information.

Obesity numbers have shot through the roof in 2015-16. Recent studies show that more than one-third or 93.3 million U.S. adults are obese. Approximately 13.7 million children and adolescents in the U.S. aged two to nineteen are also obese.

Obesity-related conditions include heart disease, stroke, type two diabetes and certain types of cancer. Obesity is one of the leading causes of preventable death.

The estimated health care costs of obesity-related illness are a staggering $190.2 billion or nearly 21% of the annual medical spending of the U.S.

In 2018, an estimated 5.8 million Americans had Alzheimer's disease. Approximately 200,000 individuals younger than age 65 were found to have early-onset Alzheimer's. One in three cases of Alzheimer's is said to be preventable through the choice of a healthy lifestyle.

Alzheimer's is not one condition, but several. They are driven by different mechanisms and typically manifest in different ways and at different ages. But all are dramatically influenced by imbalances in 36 metabolic factors that can trigger "downsizing" of the brain. New advances in rebalancing these mechanisms by adjusting lifestyle factors, including micronutrients, hormone levels, stress, and sleep quality are showing great promise.

You've only been given one body to live in. It's up to you to make it and keep it in the best running condition possible. Educate yourself on proper nutrition, and in how and when to exercise. Take advantage of the latest information on prevention. How you individually take control of your physical body is important. *Now* is the time to take action!

Number of deaths by cause, World, 2017

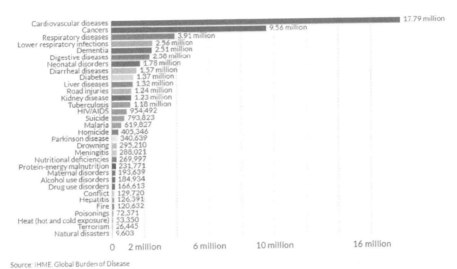

Source: IHME, Global Burden of Disease

Dr. C. Everett Koop, Former U.S. Surgeon General reminds us—

"Of the 2.4 million deaths that occur in the United States each year, 75 percent are the result of avoidable nutritional factor diseases".

As the graph on the next page shows—

The alarming fact is that foods – fruits, vegetables, and grains – now being raised on millions of acres of land, no longer contain enough of certain needed nutrients, and are starving us — no matter how much we eat of them."

Number of deaths by risk factor, World, 2017

Total annual number of deaths by risk factor, measured across all age groups and both sexes.

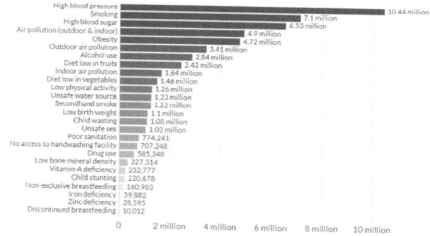

Source: IHME, Global Burden of Disease (GBD)

Without adequate nutrition, especially minerals, research has shown that people develop chronic health conditions.

More and more nutritional studies have linked many of today's most prevalent, life-threatening chronic diseases—diabetes, heart disease, stroke, obesity, high blood pressure, macular degeneration, bone loss, dementia—to nutritional deficiencies.

The simple truth may be that susceptibility to disease is linked to either toxicity from fertilizers and pesticides, or nutritional deficiency. Increasingly, scientific research has shown that the secret to lifelong health is good nutrition.

"If we could give every individual the right amount of nourishment and exercise, not too little and not too much, we have found the safest way to health."

—Hippocrates

Free Online Health Assessment

I want to offer a free gift from me to serve you and your family. In fact, feel free to share this with all you know. It is a 12-page personal health report. When you go to *https://FreeIDLifeAssessment.com* it takes you to a HIPAA compliant website. HIPAA means that nobody will see this information other than you and the computer. It will take you five to eight minutes to answer up to 28 questions. At the end of that, you can print a 12-page personal health report. It'll give you recommendations as to how to help certain portions of your life. It might suggest more sleep. It might suggest more vegetables. It's *free* and there is no obligation to do anything but take it and evaluate the information it delivers.

One of the biggest issues I've had with this is getting people to take this free questionnaire. That's right. There are people working to invest in you if you, allow it to happen.

Do you understand that you can take your life-changing events and turn them into defining moments? You can go from this point forward and start doing the things you've been called to do. Obtain the knowledge you need to get, and keep learning. Start doing the things that are available to you now, because there's no more denying it—you're infinitely capable. I've already shared that with you, so don't forget this.

If you take advantage of that personal health report, it will also make a recommendation on products they advise for you. These are products that my medical team felt helped me come through my stroke without any residual damage. Because I had been caring for my body prior to the stroke, my body was ready to take the hit. My body was prepared. In the ICU, my doctor said, "You're the healthiest sick guy I've ever seen."

Sixty-four percent of all Americans will suffer from a heart-related issue. Thirty percent of those people won't even know they had an issue. What that means is, out of ten of you reading this material, six of you will have a heart-related issue, and two of you will be dead before you even know it. Here's the other point. Eighty percent of this is preventable. Use your temple. Live a healthy lifestyle.

Achieve Financial Freedom

The second A in B.A.L.A.N.C.E. stands for Achieve Financial Freedom.

You have to do everything you possibly can to create as much wealth as you possibly can. You are infinitely capable and able. If you don't do this, you are leaving your potential untapped. It is up to you to use all your God-given talents and abilities to generate your best possible life and financial position.

You have been granted the opportunity to use whatever your highest source has given you to the fullest and to be of service to each and every one of us in exchange. If we had everybody providing value to the next person, value would be returned back to you guaranteed. If you don't have enough money and need more money, provide more value. Continue to provide value to people and the rest will take care of itself. It's just that simple.

This comes partially from what I call *the money talk*. The money talk happened in late August of 2003, in Toronto, Canada, when I was speaking at Parker Seminars. If you will recall, from earlier in the book (page 68), I shared the first part of a story where Jack Canfield and Mark Victor Hansen, the co-creators of *Chicken Soup for the Soul*®, approached me after my presentation.

Basically, I was harshly reprimanded for staying in my corporate job instead of becoming a professional speaker. Jack said I was being selfish and robbing, even cheating humanity by not using my talents. Talk about being smacked in the heart! It was obviously exactly what I needed. More importantly, I will be forever grateful to Jack Canfield for calling me out and putting me on the path I am on to this day. Thank you, Jack!

This life-changing lesson continued as Jack said, "You have the obligation to use your gifts fully and make as much money as you possibly can." Of course, as soon as he said that, I became indignant.

I hadn't received his message well and responded, "See, all of you speaker guys, it's all about the money with you." Boy, was I about to learn one of the greatest lessons of my life!

Jack went on to say, "You think this is about the money? This isn't about the money. This is about the two things that having money allows. Number one, *when you have money, you have influence.* You can make the changes you want to see in the world. Number two, *you can do things with the money to make that positive impact.* It's not about the money. It's about the two things that come with the money and the tremendous amount of good you can do with it when you use it to serve others.

This is easily one of, if not the most important, lessons I have ever learned. Therefore, we all have an obligation to make as much as we possibly can. Not for the sake of the money itself, but for how we can put that money to use to further the good on the planet.

I don't particularly like the word, obligation. Does anybody want to be obligated? I didn't think so. I like the word, invitation. Let me give you the invitation to make as much money as you possibly can. Not just for the money, but for the things that you can do with that money. Think about the changes you can make, the improvements you can do, and the fact that you can give others a hand up rather than a handout.

Everyone has their own definition of financial freedom. Personally, mine is having the financial wherewithal to do what I want, with whom I want, wherever I want, and whenever I want!

People might say to me, well, you've had a lot of money and then you went broke and then you had a lot of money again and then you went broke and now you and have a lot of money, once again. Yeah true, but I've played full-out and had a bunch of fun in the process. Peggy and I have experienced a lot of really great times and been to awesome places. One quick recommendation is, don't do or stay on the broke side. The broke side is really no fun. It puts a lot of undue pressure on you in many ways. Enough said, right? You get it.

What I truly want to do is: I want to make so much money that we can give scholarships to people in the form of entrepreneurial education, so that we can give others the opportunity to live out their dreams and visions. There are plenty of people who have a desire to contribute to humanity. Let's all do our part to facilitate their contributions.

My belief is that we have to stop the handouts but encourage the hand ups wherever and whenever possible. Let's help as many people as we can. There still has to be an *exchange of value*. If everything becomes a dead-end handout, neither you, nor anyone else will receive any value for it. To *give people a chance to live out their highest vision* is another principle I learned from my time with Jack Canfield.

What's happened in our society is there are so many people getting handouts with no value in exchange. Many people take the path of least resistance. What this means is people are basically lazy. When you give people free stuff, people take free stuff. Then, when you ask them to be accountable and responsible for the free stuff, they get upset. In my opinion that's wrong.

Jim Rohn said it this way, "Formal education will make you a living. Self-education will make you a fortune!"

We need to take responsibility for where we are in this whole thing. There has to be an exchange of value. Has this been a valuable time for you so far? Yes? Absolutely?

It's about an exchange of value. Value does not only go one way. It goes both ways.

Why Improve Your Financial Status?

Far too many people today have fallen into having a microwave mentality in a crockpot world. They live for instant gratification and many times accept long-term consequences for short-term events or pleasure. This creates multiple streams of debt.

Beyond some potentially misguided choices, financial hardships can be caused by things such as job loss or out-of-state transfer, reduction in hours or rate of pay, illness or disability affecting you or someone in your immediate family, divorce or other marital difficulties, or being called to active duty as a member of a military reserve unit. Unfortunately, many times a number of issues come together at once to create the perfect storm.

It's not usually the lack of finances that causes the divorce, but the lack of compatibility in the financial arena. Similarly, financial stress can lead to multiple physical issues like headaches, backaches, ulcers, increased blood pressure, depression, and anxiety, just to name a few.

No matter what the cause of the financial hardship, debt is typically the lingering effect and heavy weight around too many people's necks.

Let's Look at the Numbers

The average U.S. household credit card debt stands at $16,061 based on federal reserve statistics and other governmental data. By the end of 2018, total consumer debt was tracking at $4 trillion dollars. That translates to each American owing approximately 26 percent of their income to credit card debt and another 10 percent to other debts excluding car loans, and student or personal loans.

Americans have consistently piled up more debt since 2013 even though disposable income has risen during the same timeframe. Even with income rising, America's appetite for excess spending continues. Therefore, they continue to borrow more and more money, and are doing so more often.

The biggest reason most people believe Americans are not changing their credit-related behavior is because they are becoming more and more *financially illiterate*. Americans lack the fundamental knowledge in areas of basic finance and investment. When you don't understand the basics, easily obtainable money looks good and may explain part of the growing numbers in consumer borrowing.

To learn more about consumer debt and more importantly, how to manage it properly, you have to first understand what consumer debt is and what role it plays in our banking systems.

What is Consumer Debt?

By definition, consumer debt is the personal debt that an individual owes to an organization, like a bank or credit union. Many times, this type of debt is used for household purchases or transactions for non-business use. It is typically not associated with a company owing money to another company.

Another characteristic is that these purchases are usually consumable items that do not depreciate like an auto or home. This allows a purchaser to be able to obtain a significantly-priced product without having to pay the entire purchase price upfront.

There are two types of consumer debt, revolving credit and non-revolving credit.

Revolving Consumer Debt

The most common example of this type of consumer debt is credit card debt. This kind of debt is referred to as revolving, because it is meant to be paid off frequently, and typically within a month.

Revolving credit fluctuates with consumer use and usually, it comes with a variable interest rate.

Non-Revolving Consumer Debt

Conversely, non-revolving consumer debt may or may not be on a particular payment schedule. Instead, payments may be seen as fixed and are usually active for the life of the underlying asset. This type of consumer debt may include long-term loans for cars and education.

These debts typically include a fixed payment plan with few changes to the amount charged. It is possible for consumers to choose between fixed and variable interest rates for these debts in some cases. The following statistics come from the Federal Reserve's Consumer Credit G.19 release:

- ✓ Total consumer debt totaled $3.898 trillion in 2018, a 7.6 percent increase from the previous year.

- ✓ Average consumer debt per capita is approximately $11,880 (total consumer debt/total U.S. population as of July 4, 2018).

- ✓ Total revolving consumer debt was $1.039 trillion in 2018.

- ✓ Total revolving consumer debt rose 11.4 percent annually in 2018.

- ✓ Average revolving debt per capita is approximately $3,167 (total revolving consumer debt/total U.S. population as of July 4, 2018).

- ✓ Credit card debt in May 2018 broke the previous record of $1.02 trillion set in 2008.

- ✓ Credit card debt was 27 percent of total consumer debt in 2018, down from 38 percent in 2008.

- ✓ Two in ten adults say they roll over $2,500 or more a month in credit card debt. [Source: NFCC]

- ✓ Total non-revolving consumer debt was $2.858 trillion in 2018.

- ✓ Auto loans totaled $1.113 trillion in 2018.

- ✓ Student loans totaled $1.524 trillion in 2018.

- ✓ Average loans per student equal approximately $76,468 (total student loans/total students enrolled in public or private universities in 2018).

Do You See Why Financial Literacy Is So Important?

You don't have to be an economist to understand the daily mounting pressure being heaped onto individuals, corporations, and government concerning debt in our country. The due date on all this debt is coming. Sticking your head in the ground will not work. Denial is not a strategy.

Each of us, me included, needs to get smarter when it comes to money, investment, and our economy. We all play a part in this. We either feed into the economy or pull from the economy. In either case, we have some responsibility to not only ourselves, but to our fellow man and woman as well. To learn more go to: *http://BeFinanciallyFitToday.com*

Nurture Your Relationships

The N in B.A.L.A.N.C.E. stands for Nurture Your Relationships.

This is your family and social side. One of the best things you can ever do is to surround yourself with amazing people. I applaud you for picking up this material. You have worked to surround yourself with good, solid people. When you have good, solid people around you, it's amazing what can happen from it. You can learn. You can reach. You can grow. You can exchange thoughts. You can craft ideas. All sorts of amazing things happen.

There's one concept I want you to hold boldly in your memory. There's no such thing as a 50-50 relationship. It has to be a 100-100 relationship. When it's not 100-100, let's say it's 100-0, there's still 100 somewhere out there that's being wasted or not contributing.

Let me share a visual that I learned a long time ago. Imagine we have a river. There is a tall tree on each side of the river. You take each tall tree and bring it up to the midpoint, or the 50-50 point in the river, and lash those two trees together to form a bridge. However, it is a tremendously weak bridge. The bulk of the two trees are not supporting each other, only just the tips. They're bound together only by the lashings. There really isn't any strength.

This is what's happening with our marriage rate in this country. It's 50-50. Why aren't marriages working? Because the lashing releases. It has become very easy to bail out. Unfortunately, most of these marriages weren't very secure in the first place.

If you take the same tree and you bend it all the way over to the other side, then you take the second tree and bend it over to the other side, lashing them together at the midpoint and quarter points, now both trees are 100-100 together. They're an impenetrable bridge. Because you lashed the bulk of each tree together, nothing can ever happen to them. The strength is there, and an unbreakable bond is formed.

Many times, people sit and talk about how unfair things are after having given 100 percent in a relationship. Get over it. Let me just tell you right up front—spoiler alert—life isn't fair. As soon as you don't care whether it is or isn't fair, your life gets better. It doesn't matter what's fair and what's not fair. You should only care about having an amazing life experience. The way you have an amazing life experience is you push into all the areas of your life, all-in.

What you will find is that character is exposed, regardless of which stage your relationship is in. Your character doesn't necessarily change. Money or success can simply expose who you are. If you're a jerk and all of sudden you have a bunch of money, all this typically means is now, you're a jerk with a lot of money. If you're a good person with or without, now you have something worthwhile. T. Harv Eker said it this way, "How you do anything is how you do everything!" The fact of the matter is, a successful life is not made up of 50-50 relationships. It's 100-100 relationships, with each party committed to pushing all-in and giving it everything they have that is worth keeping. Love people 100-100.

When my children were still very young, I came home from a business trip only to have my ex-wife say, "I want you out."

I asked, "What did I do?"

She responded, "Nothing, I just don't love you anymore."

I said, "We have a 28-month old and a 10-month old."

She replied, "I know. Better to be from a broken home than in a broken home." I didn't know our home was broken.

Through those years of marriage, I didn't pay attention well enough. I truly "didn't know what I didn't know!" But I can assure you, I went to counseling for the next two years. I went 18 months longer than my counselor said I needed to or wanted me to. She told me I didn't need to be there anymore to which I replied, "With all due respect, I'll tell you how long I'm going to be here. This is never happening to me again!"

My approach was to make sure *I was fixed* because the dissolution of that marriage had to be connected to something I did or didn't do. Any time anything happens in a relationship, good or bad, it is worth taking a critical look to explore what could have been done better.

I took responsibility for my part in the divorce. It was not easy. It was not fun. During that time, I made a bunch of different mistakes as my kids grew up.

Life is a constantly evolving set of circumstances and decisions. Set your intentions to live the best life possible and create some accountability to ensure you stay on track.

My daughter is now 31 years old. About six months ago, we had dinner. She said, "Daddy, I just want you to know I've always loved you, but there were a whole lot of times I didn't like you much." You know how cool it is to have your daughter say that to you? Now she loves me *big time*!

The fact is, no matter what's happened in your life, you can get your life back if you want it. Can you appreciate that? My kids and I faced some challenges as they grew up. The one thing I can tell you for sure, to this day, is I am still working to grow up to be as great as my kids have turned out! There were years where I didn't know how to be a parent. My fault. Back in the day, they didn't write books on how to be a great parent. This is just another reason to always be willing to learn and grow.

I still remember my ex-wife asking me, "Don't you know how to hold a baby?"

I looked at her and said, "No, I really don't!" Where would I have learned this? I was the youngest child. She grew up as the oldest child taking care of her brothers and sisters.

Back in those days, she'd say, "Come on, you don't care". It was not that I didn't care. Truth be told, I didn't know I wasn't caring about what I needed to care about. You "don't know what you don't know" until you know it. We all have blind spots.

Who Would You like to Meet?

A few years ago, I was having dinner with a group of friends when the person sitting across from me asked, "If you could meet anyone dead or alive right now, who would it be?"

Without any delay I said, "Sir Richard Branson. I love his approach to business and life!"

The gentleman said, "No problem, I can make that happen in 62 days!"

"What?" I exclaimed. "You're kidding me, right?" He wasn't kidding! He went to work on it immediately and he had it set up. I received an invitation to the Virgin Unite charity event called, Rock the Kasbah.

This was an amazing example of knowing both the power and contents of your *contact list,* since one of your most valuable business and personal assets are your relationships with others. Everyone deserves to be respected, honored, and shown dignity throughout your interactions. Nurturing relationships is not a part-time job. It is a full-time career if you want to provide an exchange of value to all your relationships.

Rock the Kasbah

The Rock the Kasbah event was amazing. Virgin Unite held an event with about 1,500 in attendance. The purpose was to raise money to support underprivileged kids in Southeast Asia. Here are a couple of interesting *Nurture Your Relationships* stories from this event.

Earlier in the day, as I was riding the elevator down to the lobby to head out to a meeting, I was joined part of the way down by a nice, blonde young lady dressed to go for a run. Just to have some fun I said, "Hey, would you do me a favor?"

She kind of looked at me funny and said, "Sure, I guess so."

I told her, "I have to get off to a meeting this morning, so I don't have time to work out. Can you run a little bit extra today, to work out a little for me, too?"

She kind of laughed and said, "Sure" once again. It was simple enough and, in the spirit, to break the ice on a fairly long elevator ride. I was pretty sure neither of us thought too much about it at the time.

That night, at the Rock the Kasbah event, I saw the same woman, now immaculately dressed in a long evening gown. As fate would have it, my friend introduced me to her. Jean was her name. We had a quick little laugh after I thanked her for working out for me earlier. When I asked her what her relationship was to the event, she said, "I'm the Executive Director of Virgin Unite and I'm responsible for this entire event."

Wow. Who would have ever thought? It just so happened that she was actually one of the people I wanted to meet. Breaking the ice in a light-hearted fashion is a great way to start a relationship.

Having fun, enjoying myself, and working to bring a smile to another person's face turned into meeting someone who I had a desire to work with going forward. It's amazing how being friendly works!

The second story from that evening was equally as interesting. After being formally introduced to Sir Richard Branson and spending a little time talking with him one-on-one, I thought I'd excuse myself so others could have their opportunity to meet and talk with him too. As I turned to walk away, I noticed this lovely older lady, beautifully dressed in a flowing black gown with bright pink accents, sitting all by herself at a table ten feet away.

No one was talking to her, so I thought, *What the heck, I might as well go introduce myself and say hi.* When I walked over, I said, "My, you look lovely this evening. My name is Scott."

She looked up, took my hand and said, "Hi, my name is Eve."

Making small talk I asked, "What brought you out to such a wonderful event?"

Eve replied, "Richard, is my son. This event is to support my charity."

I was shocked. "What? You're Eve Branson? Sir Richard Branson's mother?" Yes, she was! Eve asked me to sit and join her for a while. She and I spent the next hour chatting. She shared *little Richie* stories with me. What an amazing time!

I share this with you because my encouragement to you is to not form any preconceived notions about people. Do not judge them as to what they can do for you or size them up for what you believe you can get from them. Show everyone the *respect, honor, and dignity* they deserve as a human being on this planet. Create true, open, long-lasting relationships by exploring their needs, their wants, their desires. First see if there is any way that you can become an asset to them.

A.S.S.E.T. is another acronym I love. By the way, teaching with acronyms is great, because if you can remember the acronym, you can usually remember the lesson! So, A.S.S.E.T. stands for becoming *A Spontaneous Servant Every Time!* When you are a spontaneous servant, you work to help others before determining whether or not they may be able to help you. This goes back to the concept of *high intention* and *low attachment*.

It also follows another great premise of *be interested, not just interesting!* Truly be interested in the other person, their life, their work, and their hobbies. Tell your story second. Encourage the other person to tell you all about themselves first, before you tell them about you and your activities.

Utilize the Tools That Are Available!

Have you ever noticed how productive some entrepreneurs and small business owners are? Others seem helpless when it comes to finding their "perfect prospect"? Some have it down growing their businesses, increasing revenues, enjoying their profits, all while spending extra time with family and friends. And the others? As they say...they are experiencing... "not so much!"

What's the secret of those enjoying extra time, energy, and money? Typically, they have discovered and are utilizing tools that the others are not. One such business-building opportunity comes from long-time friend and Queen Bee herself, Tonya Hofmann.

Tonya is and has been a master connector for years. We're much the same in this respect. Having a web and app development background, Tonya felt there had to be a better way of *"meeting the connected."* Why are they called connected? Because they have consistently performed above market expectations, have earned the trust of others, and share their connections for the greater good *when* appropriate.

Not only does Tonya's platform put the connections together, but it creates an environment in which high quality people match their products, goods, and services with the exact prospects that need, want, and desire them. It is literally becoming a match made in heaven...or by some tremendously robust algorithms that match prospect's needs with vendor supply.

Tonya says it this way, "It like Dating-Software for the Business World!" She has incorporated a rating system to insure members consistently add value to each other. There is also a significant amount of training from a group of "the best of the best" category experts designed to help grow your business, profits, you name it!

I signed up the day I learned about it...it's already paying huge dividends! To learn more, please visit: *http://JoinBeeKonnected.com*

When nurturing your relationships, information is king or queen! The more you know about the people you have some type of relationship with, the deeper the relationship can be. Spoiler alert – people like to talk about their favorite subject for the vast majority of the conversation. And that favorite subject you ask? Them! That's right, people love to talk about themselves, hear about themselves, and congratulate themselves. You get the idea.

Science details why using a contact management app on your phone is so important. For my generation and older, we were always taught to learn and retain information. Our brains were our hard drives. Gen Xers to a certain extent, and millennials specifically, are the first generations that have been taught to obtain and hold that information differently.

Where baby boomers and beyond gained knowledge and held it *internally*, younger generations like millennials have been taught to obtain information and then store it for recall *externally*. In other words, their phone, tablet, laptop, or computer has become the storage device for vast amounts of critical information. Millennials have become masterful at searching external storage devices and pulling up the necessary information at the immediate point of need, which seems to be prior to walking up and talking to someone they have met previously.

Here's the bottom line. In either case, whether you are a boomer or a millennial, at the point in the conversation where it is appropriate to say something that validates the depth and level of your relationship with the person you are talking to, those who can share and demonstrate they know personal and long-lost details about the other person garner greater and deeper relationships than those who know less about the other person. Deep down, people want you to become their cheerleader, even for those few moments!

So my friend, Adrian Chenault, a younger than boomer, developed an awesome app called, Contact Mapping *http://LearnAboutCM.com* to help anyone become an expert on the person being talked to. His app holds the critical and many times minute details that can make the person you are talking with tremendously comfortable with you. As the old axiom says, "People don't care how much you know until they know how much you care!"

Even though as a boomer, I have always worked diligently to obtain, learn, and retain this information about others, I have personally found tremendous value in having the app on my phone. I have 4,347 contacts *mapped* in my phone! In days of old, it used to be said that a person had a minimum of 250 contacts stored in their head. Because of the depth of relationships with those 250 people, anyone could be tremendously successful in business and in life because of *The Power of Your Who*. If you haven't yet read about *The Power of Your Who*, check out Bob Beaudine's book soon.

Today, because of the speed with which information is disseminated, and the reach we all have available through the World Wide Web, it makes sense to hold dear the information of your closest 250 people internally, and store the other 4,000+ externally on your phone. Go to *http://LearnAboutCM.com* for more details about this.

Nurturing Your Relationships is critical to your ongoing success and fulfillment. Depth of relationships *creates trust* in you and in your relationships. People do business with those they know, like, and trust. People date those they know, like, and trust. People marry those they know, like, and trust! The strength of relationships can be directly tied to your interest, understanding, and desire to show you care about the other person.

Becoming a Leader

I encourage you to understand that if you want people to follow you and you want to be a leader, you have to be *lead-worthy*. Be somebody who others want to follow. Be someone who helps others feel great about themselves. Why would they want to follow you? If you don't provide value in their lives, why would others want to follow you? Because everybody else is? You have to provide value in people's lives. You have to nurture relationships, being one who others look to for wisdom and guidance.

Two Books I Suggest You Purchase and Read

If you truly want to continue to learn more about *Nurturing Your Relationships*, I encourage you to purchase two of Dr. Gary Chapman's books.

The first is *The Five Love Languages* and the second is the lesser known, *The Five Apology Languages*. Why you may ask? It's pretty simple why. These two books are easy to read, easy to absorb, and most importantly, easy to put into action in your life.

The Five Love Languages talks about everyone having one dominant love language. And when you know what it is, and speak to others in their dominant love language, an amazing depth of relationship can be achieved. Isn't that what we all are actually searching for?

The five love languages are: 1) Words of Affirmation; 2) Quality Time; 3) Receiving Gifts; 4) Acts of Service; and 5) Physical Touch. Interestingly, when I spent the better part of six years on the road from Sunday to Friday, it was amazing to show the beautiful Ms. Peggy four out of the five love languages, even from the road.

To give you an example of how I put these love languages into action, I would call Peggy multiple times a day to assure her how much I loved her and cared about her using words of affirmation. Typically, once a week, I would have flowers delivered or a small gift while I was out of town. This was my practicing the love language of receiving gifts, by sending gifts. When I arrived back home, I would take care of the *honey-please-do* list, which is acts of service. And to this day, when I'm home, I rub her back every night before we go to sleep practicing physical touch.

The reality was, Peggy's primary love language was the fifth one, quality time. Because I was usually on the road, the one way she wanted to experience love was the only one I could not share. Recognizing her main love language and my inability to provide it from the road was one of the determining factors in modifying how I do business and how much I travel.

The Five Apology Languages are equally as important to know and act on. They are: 1) Expressing Regret; 2) Accepting Responsibility; 3) Making Restitution; 4) Genuinely Repenting; and 5) Requesting Forgiveness. Again, not too hard to see how valuable these can be in your ongoing relationships. Knowing how and when to apologize is extremely important. These two books are well worth the purchase!

Contribute Beyond Self

The C in B.A.L.A.N.C.E. stands for Contribute Beyond Self.

This is your giving back that also establishes part of your legacy. What do you want people to say about you? More importantly, how do you want people to feel about you? When I meet anyone, I want to be an asset to them. Asset is a five-letter acronym for *a spontaneous servant every time*. I want to be a spontaneous servant every time I meet somebody.

The chances of your needing to retain me or my services for coaching, training, or speaking the first time we meet is maybe 5 percent. However, the chances of your needing to know somebody I know, or know something I know is probably 95 percent. Become an asset to the other person. Serve them. Position yourself in that place of service. I want to be known as the clearinghouse for information and connections.

I shared this story earlier, but it's worth a quick review. One of my clients became tremendously upset one day and she said, "I am so mad."

"That's unlike you. You don't normally get mad. Why are you so mad?" She said that *Fifty Shades of Grey* was outselling her book by a ridiculous amount, and that it was junk.

I told her, "I don't know. I haven't read it."

She then replied, "But it doesn't have anything of value in it, and my book is full of value."

So, I asked her, "Do you want fame or impact?"

"What?" she was confused.

I repeated my question, "Are you out for fame or for impact?"

"Well, impact."

"So then, why are you upset?" I encouraged her to reflect on what was going on behind her emotions.

"What do you mean?" she asked.

"What if you only sold one of your books?"

"That would be terrible."

"Wait," and I paused for a moment. "What if you sold one of your books, and it was to the woman who became the next Mother Teresa?" She said, "That would be awesome."

"So, do you want fame, or do you want impact?"

This time, my client confidently said, "I want impact!"

"Then stop focusing on the trappings of fame. Did Mother Teresa want fame or want impact? Impact. When she created enough impact in the world, what happened? She became famous. Do you understand that Mother Teresa spent most of her time traveling on private jets? She didn't own them. The fact of the matter is, when you create enough impact, those who have the resources will come to serve you as you serve others."

Do you want fame, or do you want impact?

I Want to Positively Impact 1 Billion Lives on the Planet!

Not long ago, while doing a radio interview, the radio host asked me what I wanted to accomplish most in my life. This is what I said, "That's simple! It may sound lofty but I want to positively impact one billion lives on this planet." He thought that was ridiculous. "Why is this ridiculous? It's only one out of seven people. I think it's a horrible ratio."

"You're being flippant about this."

"No, I'm not," I assured him, "I should be able to touch one out of every seven lives I come across. If Facebook can hit half a billion people a day, why can't I hit a billion people in a career? What if I miss it and I only hit 100 million? Or I'm terrible at it and I hit 10 million. Or I'm really bad and I only hit a million. Would that be okay?"

"That'd be awesome," he answered.

I continued, "Well, I've already spoken to over a million people in my career. So now, I'm working on the next level." Do you understand what I'm trying to say? You can't get to the billion if you don't start with the first one standing in front of you.

Remember, two times two, times two, times two, 32 times, touches everybody on this planet. Everybody wants the entire planet. But nobody wants the first two. The first two is where the real work is. Do you understand? If two of you come out of here lit on fire to be entrepreneurs in conscious businesses, those which create and use for-profit businesses to support non-profit partners, something good has been done through this work. Now, if it is more of you, it's even better. That's what you do.

Not everybody is going to like what I say throughout this material. Not everybody is going to like the way I do it. I can't win you all. I'd like to, but that's not my concern. My concern is to win the ones I'm talking to. Be present in your conversations and win those in front of you. Don't be trying to go to the next conversation. Finish this one first.

If you haven't read Andy Andrews' book, *The Butterfly Effect*, please do. To give you a little spoiler alert, it basically says that when a butterfly flaps its wings halfway across the world, the impact of that butterfly flapping its wings affects you wherever you are today. The point Andy was making is that the smallest movement, positive or negative, sends energy around the world to change or modify what is happening. Thinking about it, do we really have to take such dramatic action all the time? Not really.

Sharing the stage with Deepak Chopra, he spoke about his take on this concept from his perspective. He said that every time we breathe out and we breathe back in, I breathe out some of me and I breathe in some of you, and you and I become one. Deepak went into much more detail, but that's basically how he broke down his way of looking at this concept.

The point is we're all here for each other. We have to lift each other up. If we do this in conscious business, we can create a new culture and a new model. We can say that people can get along. It doesn't matter what color we are. It doesn't matter what creed we are. Any of that stuff really doesn't matter.

Talking with Giants Came About Because of Lack!

Earlier in this work, I told you a little bit about how I ended up writing *Talking with Giants!* To recap, as Cynthia Kersey made an impassioned plea to support her project for Habitat for Humanity, it hit my heart unlike anything ever before. She was looking for a check to support her work. I couldn't write a check, but it did not mean I could do nothing.

So, what could I do? I utilized my relationships with some pretty awesome friends like Jack Canfield, Mark Victor Hansen, T. Harv Eker, and Cynthia Kersey. I interviewed them, wrote their stories, and shared how they all supported a charity of their own. I explained why we should support them and the charities written about in the book. I couldn't write a check, but I could write a book that turned into checks from the moment it was published in 2007 until today.

What's the point? Just because you can't do what someone asks of you doesn't mean you can't do something! Have a servant's heart and help a brother or sister out!

Random Acts of Kindness That Make a Positive Impact

While I'm thinking about this, let me share a few more ideas of things you can do with thoughtfulness, and not necessarily a bunch of money, to make a difference in people's lives. Let me give you a few techniques. Are you game for this? Instead of using the word, *technique,* let's rename it to *fun things I do.* Here are the fun things I do:

Smile – Right after I was released from the hospital after my stroke, I was not permitted to fly for a few weeks. So, I was driven to Las Vegas to rest and recuperate at my sister-in-law's house. Janet and Peggy had driven up from Los Angeles to Las Vegas, so I joined them a few days later.

In an attempt to get out of the house and do something somewhat normal, Peggy and I went to the grocery store. I figured I could push around the cart while Peggy picked out and chose our purchases. At one point, a lady came down our aisle. Just being happy to be alive, I smiled at her. She looked at me, made this funny face, turned around, and walked back up the aisle.

We went around to the second aisle, and there was another lady. I thought I'd smile at her. She saw my smile, and immediately buried her head into the ingredients on the can label in front of her.

We turned into the third aisle. Another lady was walking down the aisle, so I waited until she came next to the cart I was pushing. I flung the cart across the aisle blocking her way. Then, I smiled. Startled, she asked, "What are you doing?"

I said, "I was just discharged from the hospital and I'm pretty happy about it. I just thought I'd smile."

With that she said, "Congratulations, can I give you a hug?" She topped my smile with her hug. It was awesome! Smile or even hug someone heart to heart. They will appreciate it! At the very least, they will wonder what the heck you're up to!

Stop and Say Thank You – The credit for this idea goes to the amazing Mr. Sean G. Murphy. Virtually every time Sean and I are together, he will find somebody to stop and say thank you to.

It typically sounds something like this, "Let me take the opportunity to stop and say thank you for all the people you have served today that haven't said thank you. I appreciate who you are and what you've done and just wanted to say thank you!"

If I've seen Sean do this once, I've seen him do it hundreds of times. He makes me want to be a better person! The look on the faces of those on the receiving end is absolutely priceless. Like so many kind acts, this is really simple to do, and it costs nothing. These small, extra gestures truly brighten everyone's day.

Answering Your Phone – Let's say someone named, Nikki, calls me. I'll answer the phone something like this, "Nikki's fan club?" True? Absolutely! That's the way I answer the phone. When I see a name pop up on my caller ID, I'll answer using their name. "Bill Anderson's fan club?" It always changes how we start the conversation. There's always a little chuckle. There's always a little fun. It doesn't matter how serious it is.

How you choose to answer your phone is up to you. You might as well have a little fun in the process. Life can be a grind at times. Causing a chuckle breaks the seriousness and lightens the mood. Life and business have plenty of challenges daily. Controlling this little portion of your interactions makes a huge difference for such a simple strategy.

Responding to Others/The First Contact – This concept links back to the legendary Zig Ziglar. If you ever had the pleasure to meet Zig, and if you ever asked Zig how he's doing, virtually every time Zig's answer would be, "Better than good!" Actually, it's more like, "*Betteeeerrr than goooood!*" He set a positive tone for every conversation.

Being a fan of positive conversations, many years ago I adopted the concept of creating my own initial responses. For those I've had the honor to meet personally, more than likely, if you asked me a question like, "How are you today?" You would have been the recipient of,

"Fabulous, but I'll get better!"

You cannot believe how sharing "Fabulous, but I'll get better!" sets the tone and starts a conversation much differently than responding with, "I'm getting by!" or, "I'm breathing." Have you ever noticed most people don't answer in a positive way?

This becomes another way you *differentiate yourself from the masses. Be* someone people *want* to be around! Creating your own tremendously positive answers opens possibilities you may not have thought of before.

One time, walking up to the ticket counter at Dallas Fort Worth airport, the female ticket agent asked, "How are you today?"

I replied with my go-to answer, "Fabulous, but I'll get better!"

She said, "Better than fabulous? What is better than fabulous?"

To which I playfully responded, "Being upgraded for my flight."

Chuckling, she said, "I can't just upgrade you."

I said, "I didn't ask for an upgrade, I was just answering your question about what is better than fabulous?"

She paused for a moment, typed a few things into the computer, looked up and said, "Well, this is your lucky day. This flight is wide open upfront. How about I make your day better than fabulous?"

I gratefully accepted! I would have been equally as grateful if she couldn't or hadn't upgraded me. That's not why I answered as I did. I answer that way every time! The reason for creating a fun and different response than most choose to use, is to create some positive energy or at the very least, have a little fun seeing and hearing the other person's response. This is easy to put into action. Give it a whirl!

Contact List Roulette – This is one of the things that I'll do at least once or twice a week. This is a great tool when you're stuck in traffic. You can't go anywhere anyway. Pick up your phone, go to the contact section, and flick your contact list so it starts scrolling up. Whenever you feel like it, stop the scrolling and see what name your finger lands on. Then, the fun starts.

Call the number you chose and make sure to call them, right then and there. While it's always great to talk to your contacts, sometimes I hope they don't answer, and the call goes straight to voicemail. Again, this is when the fun starts. Here is an example of a message I would leave:

"Hey, this is Scott Schilling, the President of the (insert their name here) Fan Club. I'm just calling to let you know how awesome you are, and what a positive impact you make in my life and the lives of so many others. Just wanted to let you know you're a Rockstar! You're absolutely freaking awesome, and I miss you. Give me a call when you can!" Then I hang up. You cannot believe some of the return calls you get. They are awesome! More times than I can count, contacts have called back to say thank you for making their day.

The calls you get back are worth it. In the vast majority of the calls I get back, people will say that I have no idea how much they needed my voicemail at that moment. Most times, we have no idea how little it takes to make a positive impact in the lives of others. Sound fun? Nurture your relationships with people. Make a difference in people's lives. Do something new. Do something different. Differentiate yourself.

Educate Yourself Continually

The E in B.A.L.A.N.C.E. stands for Educate Yourself Continually.

This is your personal side. We are all an assimilation of the knowledge we gain and the people we associate with consistently. You and your life experiences are basically determined by who you hang out with and the books you read. If you're not where you want to be, read more books. Hang around with better people.

You are ultimately the sum total of your five closest friends. Take your five closest friends' income, add it together, and divide it by five. You will be plus or minus $10,000 of where they are, period, end of conversation.

If you want to become better in any area of life, hang around with better people. It doesn't mean don't love your friends within your present inner circle, but it does mean you should not let your friends drag you down. Not everybody is as excited about your success as you are. You need to make sure that you're excited about everything you do.

You need to go a little bit crazy and become your own biggest cheerleader. You have to understand why you do what you do. If you don't understand your why, you have an issue, because if you don't understand it, how can you share it with anybody else?

My encouragement to you is to create a *why* video. This video assembles pictures of all the things that are truly important to you in your life. It can also show the things you are striving to add to your life. My *why* video starts out showing pictures of my career, with me on stage in front of tens of thousands of people. Every time I watch the video, it takes me back to those events, the presentations, and the good that came from them.

Then, it shows numerous pictures of Peggy and me, our trips to the British Virgin Islands, the catamarans we chartered, and our fun on the beaches. It goes on to show pictures of my son, Taylor, and daughter, Jordan, in some of their greatest moments. And of course, there are plenty of pictures of Willie, the wonder puppy, in all his glory.

My *why* video then shows the various books I have written, trainings I have given, and philanthropic endeavors I have and want to be involved in. You get the idea. It is three minutes and eleven seconds of visual review and vision casting across all seven areas of life. It is all set to the music of the Newsboys in their song, "Born Again". It's invigorating to watch.

Your *why* video gives you a visual representation of why you do what you do. I suggest all of you create a *why* video. The reasons are pretty simple. Number one, it communicates why you do what you do. Number two, there's going to come a time when you will more than likely need a pick-me-up. This video will do just that. I was in six cities in eight days over the last couple of weeks. I can assure you that no matter how much you love speaking to people and helping people, you get tired. At some point, you wonder, *why am I doing this? This is crazy.*

Peggy is at home. Willie is at home. My dog misses me. My wife, too. The fact of the matter is I have that video available to play on my computer. You can sit in your hotel room, your office, wherever you are and in three and a half minutes, you can gain back the feelings and emotions of why you do what you do.

Part of my *why* video includes the day I presented in front of 25,000 people inside a huge arena. It feels cool to watch this back. It takes you back to the place where you know you are going to change a lot of lives there that day. You feel and relive those experiences. If you want to talk further about how you create a *why* video, please feel free to reach out to me for help.

This is what it comes down to: *When you have a big enough what, a strong enough why, then the how shows up!* Everybody sits there and asks, how am I going to do this? How am I going to get paid? How am I going to make this money? How? These are the wrong questions. The question leads back to when you have a big enough what you want to accomplish, a strong enough why you want to do it, then the how to do it will show up. You just have to trust this, because you're going to come across a lot of things in life that will dissuade you.

Abraham Lincoln said, "Always bear in mind, your own resolution to succeed is more important than any other one thing". Henry Ford said, "Think you can or think you can't, you're right either way!" It's all what's in your heart. If you draw from this, you have something special.

There's a Reason Millennials Think Differently

One of the reasons to continually learn more and educate yourself is to stay on top of what's happening in this new day and age. Let's talk about millennials. Yes, millennials think differently, but do you understand why?

A couple of years ago, I was at an event where the guest speaker presented the results of a study conducted at the University of Dallas. Based on evolutionary theory, it was a study that identified and concluded there have been three major changes in the physical development of the human brain since mankind began.

Believe it or not, the information revealed in this study can truly help you understand the millennial generation and even those younger than they are. It will explain why they think and act differently than any other generation to date. Here's a quick snapshot of the results.

The study basically detailed that through the history of all mankind, there have been three great events that have changed how the actual formation of the human brain occurs. It was proposed that the first was in about 750 B.C. This is when cavemen and cavewomen went from only verbal communication, like grunting, to including written communications, such as hieroglyphics on a cave wall. So, the first change was being able to process written word, as well as spoken word.

The second great change in the formation of the brain came in approximately 1440 A.D. This was tied to Guttenberg inventing the printing press. With the invention of the printing press, duplicability took place with the moveable type printing press. Now the brain had to be able to decipher spoken word, written word, and the newly and widely available printed word.

The third great change in the formation of the brain is what is responsible for the fact that millennials think and act differently than previous generations.

The third event was caused by the advent of the internet. Now the World Wide Web, added the existence of the digital word to printed word, written word, and spoken word. So why has this caused other changes in the millennials thoughts and actions you ask?

Because for the first time in history, millennials were being educated differently than previous generations. Baby boomers like me, even Gen Xers, and all previous generations have been educated to learn, absorb, and hold knowledge. That's right, to a certain extent, we are walking file cabinets of information held in our memory banks ready to be called on when needed.

The millennial generation and younger have not been taught to learn, absorb, and hold information for the most part. They have been taught to learn the information generally, understand where that information can be retrieved and reviewed digitally, and find that knowledge when needed. In other words, they have been taught to not hold knowledge unless, it was knowing the filing system and how and where to access it.

This difference, when put into action and lived out daily, is and can be a *massive* difference in how people respond and act in different situations. This topic can be an entire book in and of itself! Here's an opportunity that exists no matter what generation you hail from. Millennials who team up with older generations who hold knowledge, can gain a competitive advantage when the older generations share key information with them.

Likewise, older generations who have knowledge held internally, can energize their efforts by teaming up with millennials to leverage their knowledge of how to access, expand, and process digital information. Because of the newer knowledge of millennials and their distribution methods, you will be able to move quicker to market.

Joining the generations together can be tremendously advantageous provided you have educated yourself about why and how to work together. You will both be better for it!

The Value of Having Mentors

Experience is a great teacher. It's also a very expensive teacher. There is a proven way to gain the experience you need with far less time, expense, and pain. This is through a mentorship/apprenticeship approach. Back in the day, this was actually the only way crafts were handed down.

A mentor took in an apprentice and shared the most intricate details in whatever area of expertise they were considered to be highly skilled and knowledgeable. To this day, having a mentor or mentors is the best and fastest way to achieve competency in any given area.

Personally, I had a desire to gain expertise in a number of areas. For me, it made sense to seek out and retain the top mentor in each specific area of growth. The one thing I made clear with each of my mentors was that everything they taught me, I committed to teach to my students.

As students came to me to learn, I was dedicated to share all I had learned from the others. And that's exactly what happened. I'm proud of working with each of my mentors and to this day, these relationships have actually gone past the teacher/student relationship. We have become friends and colleagues.

So, who have I studied under? This is a long and prestigious list. When I wanted to become a professional speaker, John Childers was the man. John has trained thousands of speakers across the span of his career. I'm honored to have been the only one he had ever recommended to an organization as *the one who will make it happen* for them.

With success, the obvious choice was Jack Canfield, America's Success Coach. Jack and I have shared the stage together, have been in each other's books, and helped each other out at events whenever possible. He's also become a great friend.

When I wanted to learn the art of the Mastermind, it was the great Dr. John Carpenter Dealey. John's advisory councils are still in action, with some being around for over 30 years.

When it came to learning what to do and what not to do trading in the stock market, I've learned from multiple mentors. They are Freddie Rick, Phil Town, and Mike Coval. To this day, Mike teaches some of the most profitable strategies with the least amount of risk and effort possible.

Others who have played a role in who I am today and why I present and train the way I do include the legendary Zig Ziglar, Brian Tracy, T. Harv Eker, Mark Victor Hansen, James Smith, Dr. Clarice Fluitt, John Maxwell, Joel Osteen, Tony Robbins, Krish Dhanam, Tom Hopkins, and a fair number more.

My encouragement to you is to identify the area of expertise that truly makes your heart sing. Evaluate who the best of the best is in that particular area of expertise, enroll in their courses, create a working relationship with them, and become a sponge. If they say this is the way you do something, do it that way.

If You Want to Do What I Do, Do What I Do!

One of my favorite stories happened with my speaking mentor, John Childers. A few years ago, John flew into Dallas and called me. He invited me to dinner and said it was his treat. It was awesome to have John offer to buy, since in the past it was me writing the checks.

We went to Uncle Julio's here in Dallas. After our margaritas arrived John said, "Scott, you're easily the most successful student I've ever mentored. You've gone on to have an awesome career, but I have to ask you one question."

I said, "Sure, John, fire away."

"Out of the thousands of speakers who have completed my courses, you are the only one who has done everything I suggested you do. I have to know why?"

I answered, "John, I'd be happy to answer that for you, but let me start by asking *you* a couple of questions first."

He said, "Okay."

I asked him, "How many dollars' worth of checks have I written you over our working relationship?" John said a number. I agreed, "That sounds about right. And how many of those checks did you cash?"

"Every one of them!"

"Now, you have your answer! Why would I come to you to learn how to become a speaker and create a speaking business, and then do it differently than you told me?"

John replied, "That makes total sense."

Isn't that amazing? It was to me. People retain a mentor to learn how to shorten up the learning curve and how to launch their businesses more effectively and efficiently, and then don't do what they've been told to do.

One of my favorite lines from John pulls this section together. He said, "If you want to do what I do, do what I do!" It doesn't get much simpler than that!

Read the Book

A number of years ago, while enjoying a wonderful lunch with Zig, Jean, and Julie Ziglar, Julie looked me square in the eyes and said, "You don't know the book well enough to know what God has in store for you!" It's not totally clear how Julie knew this, but she did. That conversation and Julie's insistence that I needed to know *The Book* better made a huge impression.

Similarly, while having breakfast with Bob Beaudine, the author of two bestsellers, *The Power of Who* and *2 Chairs*. I was sharing how at an event earlier in the week, a gentleman asked for advice on how to get a prospective employer to hire him.

My suggestion to this gentleman was the next time he spoke with the employer, he should ask this one question, "What would make hiring me be the easiest decision you have ever made in your professional career?" And if what he says is ethical and moral, tell him to hire you!

Bob said, "That's a great piece of advice. Have you ever asked that question of God?" I had been sharing with Bob my desire to be used by God to help build HIS kingdom. Bob proceeded to tell me that I didn't even listen to my own coaching. Ouch, that's going to leave a mark!

I had also shared my desire to be used by God with another great friend, inspirational speaker, and marketplace minister, Krish Dhanam. Krish responded, "Wrong prayer! It is not, God use me. It is, *God make me usable!*" Let that sink in for a moment!

Now, back to my conversation with Bob…

Bob said, "Go ahead, ask me! I'll be God".

I was game so I asked, "God, what would make bringing me into the service of building your kingdom the easiest decision you've made across all of time?"

Bob came back quickly, "Read my book!"

I responded, "I watch Joel Osteen every Sunday."

Bob said again, "Read my book!"

"I watch Joyce Meyer almost every day!" I said proudly.

"Read my book!" Bob exclaimed.

"Bob, what are you trying to say?"

Patiently, he repeated for the fourth time, "Read the book!"

I went home from our meeting and I opened up my Bible. I started with Proverbs chapter one, verses one through six. As I finished up, I received a call from a friend I hadn't talked to in months. He asked me if I'd be interested in a 21-day tour with him that would pay me six-digits. I have to admit, my first thought was, "Holy cow! If this works this fast, I'm reading the whole book!" That is when I committed to read at least 30 minutes a day until I read the Bible all the way through. From August 8th to January 6th, I read the entire Bible for the first time!

To this day, I do not claim to be a grand theologian. I have, however, read more and continue to strive to learn more going forward. It is truly amazing that anything you or I have been facing in our lives is addressed here. It provides guidance and direction as to what to do. This must be why they call it, the BIBLE or Basic Instructions Before Leaving Earth.

A Little Wisdom from Zig

As Zig and I were finishing our time together in the aforementioned lunch, I said, "Zig, thank you so much for our time together. This just means the world to me".

Zig replied, "Scott, can I leave you with one last thing?"

"Absolutely, Zig. Give me a nugget."

He said, "If you're ever discouraged or lack the encouragement you need, always remember at least this one point. Even Moses was a basket case."

"Zig, you still got it," I praised.

And he said, "I always will."

That's the kind of impact we can have with people. Understand that even Moses was a basket case and he turned out pretty good. What Zig shared with me that day has been invaluable for the rest of my life. We all have the ability to positively impact our own lives and the lives of so many, provided we continue to educate ourselves. Put great things into your mind and great things will come out!

Guidelines from God

While the following passage "Guidelines from God" comes from an anonymous author, they are great words to read, absorb, and live by daily. I thought I would include them for your reflection.

Effective immediately! Please be aware that there are *changes you* need to make in *your* life. These changes need to be completed in order that I may fulfill My promises to you to grant you peace, joy, and happiness in this life. I apologize for any inconvenience, but after all that I am doing, this seems very little to ask of you. Please, follow these ten guidelines:

QUIT WORRYING: Life has dealt you a blow and all you do is sit and worry. Have you forgotten that I am here to take all your burdens and carry them for you? Or do you just enjoy fretting over every little thing that comes your way?

PUT IT ON THE LIST: Something needs to be done or taken care of. Put it on the list. No, not *your* list. Put it on *my* to-do list. Let *me* be the one to take care of the problem. I can't help you until you turn it over to me. And although my to-do list is long, I am after all...God. I can take care of anything you put into my hands. In fact, if the truth were ever really known, I take care of a lot of things for you that you never even realize.

TRUST ME: Once you've given your burdens to me, quit trying to take them back. Trust in me. Have the faith that I will take care of all your needs, your problems, and your trials. Problems with the kids? Put them on my list. Problem with finances? Put it on my list. Problems with your emotional roller coaster? For my sake, put it on my list. I want to help you. All you have to do is ask.

LEAVE IT ALONE: Don't wake up one morning and say, "Well, I'm feeling much stronger now. I think I can handle it from here." Why do you think you are feeling stronger now? It's simple. You gave me your burdens, and I'm taking care of them now. I also renew your strength and cover you in my peace. Don't you know that if I give you these problems back, you will be right back where you started? Leave them with me and forget about them. Just let me do my job.

TALK TO ME: I want you to forget a lot of things. Forget what was making you crazy. Forget the worry and the fretting, because you know I'm in control. But there's one thing I pray you never forget. Please, don't forget to talk to me *often*! I love *you*! I want to hear your voice. I want you to include me in on the things going on in your life. I want to hear you talk about your friends and family. Prayer is simply you having a conversation with me. I want to be your dearest friend.

HAVE FAITH: I see a lot of things from up here that you can't see from where you are. Have faith in me that I know what I'm doing. Trust me, you wouldn't want the view from my eyes. I will continue to care for you, watch over you, and meet your needs. You only have to trust me.

SHARE: You were taught to share when you were only two years old. When did you forget? That rule still applies. Share with those who are less fortunate than you. Share your joy with those who need encouragement. Share your laughter with those who haven't heard any in such a long time. Share your tears with those who have forgotten how to cry. Share your faith with those who have none.

BE PATIENT: I managed to fix it so in just one lifetime you could have so many diverse experiences. You grow from a child to an adult, have children, change jobs many times, learn many trades, travel to so many places, meet thousands of people, and experience so much. How can you be so impatient then when it takes me a little longer than you expect to handle something on my to-do list? Trust in my timing, for my timing is perfect. Just because I created the entire universe in only six days, everyone thinks I should always rush, rush, rush.

BE KIND: Be kind to others, for I love them just as much as I love you. They may not dress like you, or talk like you, or live the same way you do, but I still love you all. Please try to get along, for my sake. I created each of you different in some way. It would be too boring if you were all identical. Please, know I love each of your differences.

LOVE YOURSELF: As much as I love you, how can you not love yourself? You were created by me for one reason only—to be loved, and to love in return. I am a God of love. Love me. Love your neighbors. But also love yourself. It makes my heart ache when I see you so angry with yourself when things go wrong. You are very precious to me.

Don't ever forget, touch someone with your love. Rather than focus upon the thorns of life, smell the roses, and count your blessings! God bless and keep you and, have a great day!

Chapter 6

EASY STEPS THAT MAKE A DIFFERENCE

Affirmations

Affirmations are a great way to get out of your comfort zone and stretch yourself. By repeating properly constructed affirmations, you can fill your subconscious with new, positive, and encouraging thoughts. Anything we focus on consistently causes your reticular activating system (the alerting part of the brain) to be able to validate your core beliefs.

Affirmations are statements that describe what you would like to have, goals you'd like to reach, or situations you'd like to achieve. They start with "I am", are in present tense, positive, specific, include an action word ending in -ing, have emotion, are for you, and can add *or something better* at the end. Here are some examples:

I am using all things I experience to educate me!

I am using all things to make me better in all areas of life!

I am strong! I am powerful! I am intelligent!

I am handling all situations with dignity!

I am more than a conqueror!

I am improving physically every day!

I am blessed! I am prosperous! I am happy! I am healthy!

I am talented! I am creative! I am valuable! I am wise!

I am using all my God-given talents and capabilities fully!

I am fearfully and wonderfully made!

I am a servant leader!

I am a child of the Most High God!

I am becoming all God has created me to be!

I am victorious!

I am happy and whole, and I am heard!

I am calm and love surrounds me always!

I am calm and people come to me with ease in love!

I am loved, always appreciated, and supported!

I am tuned in, tapped in, and turned on at all times!

I am experiencing my friends, family, and colleagues surrounding me with love at all times!

I am receiving love and support at all times!

I am experiencing the birthright of love from my Source!

I am easily and effortlessly receiving God's love!

I am filling my cup first and then feeding the world from what overflows!

I am aligned with the fact that money gives me options!

I am completely loved, supported, and guided by many heavenly beings, and have nothing to fear.

I am keeping my thoughts positive and staying centered in my prayers and affirmations.

I am living with divine trust that everything is working out exactly aligned with a divine plan, with divine blessings for everyone involved.

Tips for Handling Specific Situations

No matter who you are, what you do professionally, or how wonderful you are personally, there are going to be ups and downs in your life. Some will be positive, some not so positive. Remember, you are not the only one facing these various situations.

Looking back to the beginning of this work, it's not the events in your life that determine the outcomes and the quality of your life. Rather, it is the combination of the events themselves with your response to those particular events that will truly determine your outcomes. Realizing this, let's put together some strategies on how to address, process, and handle a number of situations that are sure to come along at some point.

Learn to Let Go – Develop some creative outlets for your frustrations. This may include physical activities like running, swimming, lifting weights, or playing a sport. You may choose to discuss things with a friend. Sometimes just getting it off your chest feels great.

Another possibility is to go ahead and journal your thoughts and feelings. Expressing your frustrations in some manner does the soul good.

Finally, I suggest you practice forgiveness. Forgiving another person who you believe is the underlying issue always makes a positive difference.

It has been often said that *resentment is like taking poison and waiting for the other person to die.* "Forgive them for they know not what they do!"

You're Not the Lone Ranger - Realize that you are not alone in this situation. There are now over seven billion people on the planet and for you to believe that you are the only one facing this issue, just isn't true. Someone somewhere is up against the same issue as you.

Someone is feeling upset, scared, unhappy, or down and out, too. They also are wondering, "Why am I experiencing this?" Recognizing this fact should help you make the transition from victim to victor.

The good news is, because you are not alone in this, there stands the potential to find and model someone else's solution to your situation.

If they could create an approach that brought them through this issue, you may be able to parallel what they did and get through this as well.

Take advantage of the social sharing that goes on in times of need. Adopt OPS or *other people's solutions* to your advantage.

Focus on the Positive – Being upset, throwing a tantrum, or staying frustrated is not going to solve anything. The original problem that caused you to be upset will remain even after you execute some not-so-well-thought-out actions.

You'd better take a few moments to think it through calmly. You already have one issue to address. There is no particular reason to create additional issues for yourself.

Also, far too often, rash actions complicate things and rarely do they improve them. Stay focused on potential *positive* solutions as opposed to staying in the past and reliving the issue. Crying over spilled milk has never been productive.

You Control Your Choices – Recognize that *you* always have a choice. At least this is within your control. No matter what happens, you are the king or queen of your castle. Events + Responses = Outcomes
(E + R = O).

Earlier, we looked at the fact that we cannot control every event in our lives. That being said, we can control our responses to those events. Your behavior is up to you – so, choose better.

This applies whether the perceived event is positive or negative. Every time something happens in life, potential actions can come to life. My encouragement is to choose the action that supports the ultimate outcome you would prefer, rather than the action that may take you further away from your desired result.

That may seem like common sense, but as they say, many times these days, common sense is not so common. You want better outcomes, so make better choices when it comes to how you respond to particular situations.

Look at Things Objectively – Typically, no one does anything purposely to mess up. Whatever happened, happened, so the next choice you have becomes your response.

There's an old saying, "It is what it is!" Take the steam out of the situation. Remove any overly aggressive or hostile emotions. Looking at it objectively, by definition, means to look at it in a way that is not influenced by personal feelings or opinions.

Another way of saying this may be, "don't take it personally". Sometimes in life, stuff happens!

Control What You Can Control – Focus your attention on the areas you have control over. Be empowered by your own abilities. Know that nothing ever comes your way that you are not prepared to handle.

When you control what you can control, you are no longer a passive spectator in your life. Rather, you are an active participant and writing the narrative of your life.

Engage fully where and when it makes sense. You are powerful, so maintain your power. There is no reason to surrender it to anyone else.

Talk It Out – Reach out to others for help if and when you need it. It is okay to ask for help. We are only as broad as our experiences and our knowledge. More than likely, there are trained professionals who have the skills necessary to work with you.

When I was divorced many years ago, I was encouraged to work with a marriage counselor as I went through the divorce process. It became a great opportunity to identify what could have been done better or differently.

In reality, those sessions were not about working to save that marriage. They were there to ensure that I learned what issues happened, and how I addressed things as they happened. Most importantly, I needed to learn how to, hopefully, never have the same issues again in my next marriage.

Seems like we did some pretty decent work. On November 25th, I'll have been married for 24 years and counting!

You Never Are Given More Than You Can Handle – Ultimately, your trial is just a blip on the radar. See this as yet another obstacle to overcome. As a friend said long ago, the goal of life is to be constantly growing and expanding. Everything happens for a reason. See that reason as being there to serve you and your future.

The path to your goals is rarely straight and narrow. There are bumps, obstacles, obstructions, and distractions along the way. Sometimes you may have to go up, over, under, or around those obstacles.

The point is, if you want something bad enough, you need to learn how to do what it takes to accomplish your goals. Nobody ever said everything was going to be fair or easy. In reality, you probably wouldn't want it that way anyway.

Understand Everything Provides a Learning Opportunity – Because you have just lived through another situation, you now have a chance to learn from your latest experience. Experience is a great teacher. Unfortunately, many times it is a very expensive teacher. If you are going to suffer the expense, you might as well learn!

Looking at everything as a potential learning experience also keeps you in a positive frame of mind. After all, who doesn't like to learn?

Here are five questions I created for my coaching clients to help turn *any* event into a potential learning event.

1. What was the lesson learned?

2. What was the gift you received?

3. What did you do to create this situation?

4. What would you modify next time to make it better?

5. How is this going to serve you for the rest of your life?

Let's take a look at each, question-by-question using my stroke as an example situation.

1. *What was the lesson learned?* Lesson: When you get smacked in the head by the rear deck of your car, and you have a headache for eight straight days, you should go to the doctor to get checked out!

2. *What was the gift you received?* Gift: That even though I did not go to the doctor to get checked out, I am alive and well!

3. *What did you do to create it?* Action: I was trying to do too much at the same time. I was balancing a box of books, flipped open the rear deck of my SUV, flung it up too hard and too fast.

4. *What would you modify next time to make it better?* Better action: I would not throw the deck up so hard, be more careful ducking underneath it, and sell that car. Never keep a car that attacks you!

5. *How is this going to serve you the rest of your life?* Results: share this story to ultimately share these five questions. Share my story to better educate the public on the hazards of a stroke and how to prevent one. Use my story to help raise money for the American Heart and Stroke Association. So much good has already come out of it!

Keep the Faith – Remember, all things work for your good! Life is tough. No matter how much or how bad the stuff is that gets thrown your way, you can and will make it through!

God, or whatever you choose as your higher source, has a plan for your life. It's a great plan full of hope and an amazing future. Sometimes, you have to walk through the fire. The good news is, you, like me, have the ability to pass through the fire with only a hint of the smell of smoke.

Continue to *be* the amazing person you are. Know that you are wonderfully and fearfully made. Know that you are even stronger than you think or know. Keep up your awesome life! Not only for you, but for those who count on you!

Chapter 7

FORMULA FOR REINVENTING YOURSELF

A DREAM I LIVE

Along the way, I've been blessed to be associated with many brilliant mentors. These people have been there and done that, and more importantly, have been willing to pass along what they have learned. I began contemplating how I was going to share with others the wealth of information I received. After all, I was now living my dream, so the idea made sense to create a formula on how to reinvent yourself. Hopefully, this is something people can wrap their mind around. It is called, *A Dream I Live*!

As the initial part of this action plan, I'd like to cover three pivotal areas that are crucial to your new foundation. These areas are: Awareness, Deciding on Your Future, and Redesigning Your Activities.

Awareness

Awareness by definition is *to have knowledge of*. That's right, just plain old having knowledge of what's going on in your life. It is understanding what kind of effects the actions in your life are having on you, and then doing something about them to create a newer, more fabulous you. We all tend to fall into routines or take things for granted. After all, we live in such a fast-paced world and this can be an easy excuse for not being aware. It's easy for things to drop off of your personal priority list.

As a professional speaker, trainer, author, and executive coach, it became very evident that I was not living life to its fullest. The highest vision and potential God had put me here for, had not been achieved. Not because I wasn't working at it. A number of years ago, it was because I did not have my body, my physical plant, at its optimum.

My finances were also a mess. Regarding career, I hadn't taken the bull by the horns and shared the messages of hope and inspiration that I had committed to presenting from the stage on September 29th, 2012. And when you have a variety of areas in your life that are not right, many other things aren't right as well. Or, at the very least—as good as they could be.

In looking back at how *getting back on track* transpired in my life, it made a ton of sense to document it and share it with those who might be interested in regaining control of their own lives. I wanted to inspire those who had a desire to reach a higher level of fulfillment.

Today we are living in a society that wants instant gratification. So many people aren't looking ahead and at the big picture. Because of this nearsightedness, they are not realizing their life could be so much more gratifying and blessed. Many people accept what life has become. What a shame. Life could be anything and everything they want it to be, if they took action. It reminds me of the old adage, "You don't know what you don't know, until you know it".

If they had just invested more in themselves along the way, they could be even more satisfied. Contentment is a wonderful thing, but so is what I call *a positive discontent*. Contentment can actually be the enemy of living your life to its fullest. A long time ago someone shared the saying, "You are either green and growing or ripe and rotting." Who wants to be rotting? Stagnation is a terrible thing.

Positive discontent on the other hand is that inner voice that helps you strive for the next level, whatever that may mean to you. It's the part of you that keeps growing for the greater good. It is your biggest cheerleader helping you understand you can achieve even more and live a more rewarding life. It is something we all have within us once we learn to identify it and listen to it.

My realization of *positive discontent* came out of a Mastermind group in which a friend was sharing his ten rules for living life. One of his rules was *never be satisfied*. Immediately, my gut fired a message to my brain that said, "*Oh, what a shame. How do you enjoy life if you are never satisfied? That seems kind of harsh.*"

Then my intuition kicked in. How about renaming the concept in a more positive and applicable way? What came to mind was *positive discontent*. Although you won't find it in the Webster's Dictionary, here is the definition I developed. Positive discontent is a process by which you have total and unapologetic gratitude for everything in your life, while holding the accompanying positive expectation that the world has even greater things in store for you. Now, that's powerful!

It is this positive discontent which put my quest for fitness in full gear years ago. My overall life, accomplishments, fulfillment, and the zest for living, expanded enormously over this 15-month journey. It's hard to believe all the positive changes, and I'm blessed to be living it. You almost have to pinch yourself daily while saying, "I'm living my dream and it keeps getting better!"

This is all happening at a time when things aren't so chipper out in the real world for so many people. Many of the issues we are facing around the globe today are truly heartbreaking. As I see it, you can either succumb to them, or do something to improve them. Doing what you can do to improve them sounds like a whole lot more fun and gratifying to me.

As I've shared earlier in this work, one of my mentors, Jack Canfield, taught a formula for growth in any aspect of your life. It is so simple and yet, few people ever act on it. The formula is Growth = Awareness + Inspired Action. If we want to grow in any area of our lives, we must first become aware of that potential for growth and then take inspired action toward that growth.

It's hard to believe that awareness can be so elusive. With the pace and pressures of life today, many people numb out what's really going on around them. They plod through life without the passion or zest for it. It's really a shame and certainly not what we were put on earth for. I was no different. I'd love to say I wasn't, but I became as complacent as the next person. I saw the numbers on the scale, deteriorating bank balances, professional frustrations, and did very little, if anything, about them.

One day, during one of our Platinum Inner-Circle Mastermind meetings with Jack, we were doing an exercise called, *Eight Questions*. Being teamed up with Peggy Cappy, a great friend and easily the top yoga guru in the country, we started to go through the exercise. Please understand that I truly believed everything in my life was going smashingly as we started the exercise.

I share this exercise as an example that could be used in any of the seven areas of life. For me, at the time we did the exercise, it called out my need to right size my body for longevity.

Peggy asked the first question, "What's a disturbing or troubling situation in your life?"

My answer was a non-answer. "Nothing, everything is great!"

She followed with, "Nice try! But, what's a disturbing or troubling situation in your life?"

Again, I came back with, "Everything is great. I can't think of a single thing that is troubling me at the moment." Denial is an amazing thing. You don't even know you're in it until someone else calls you on it.

Peggy persisted, "You have to give me an answer. What's a disturbing or troubling situation in your life?" It was evident she was not going to let me off the hook.

Very flippantly I replied, "I'm fat!" I didn't really believe this—even more denial—but I did need to come up with something. I knew this wasn't going to go anywhere, because *fat* wasn't the way I saw myself or the way other people saw me. I was a big guy, had a large frame, and carried myself well. By the way, these are all code words and nice ways of saying you're fat!

The second question probed a little further, "How are you creating it or allowing it to happen?" That was pretty obvious.

My answer was, "I'm not recognizing it or really doing anything about it." I was still brushing off the exercise and not being serious, as if this was not a real issue in my life.

The third question was the one that hit home. Peggy asked, "What are you pretending not to know?"

My answer this time, with great resignation and a sinking heart was, "I'm fat". I was totally deflated in a matter of seconds. It was like being hit upside the head with a two by four and being kicked in the gut at the same time. Ouch, that's going to leave a mark! Deep down, being overweight and out of shape really bothered me. And I had been masking it all this time.

The fourth question produced a very quick and enlightening answer. The question was, "What is the payoff for keeping it this way?"

My answer was, "It's easy! You don't have to work out. You don't have to watch what you eat. You can do basically whatever it is that you want to do. It doesn't matter!" Did that really just come out of my mouth? Are you kidding me? Have you really considered the long-term effects? I obviously did not.

That's when the fifth question followed up what was already coming to my mind. "What is the cost for keeping it this way?"

"I could die!" I exclaimed. Where did that come from? I'd never thought about anything like this before. Talk about getting your attention and gaining some really quick awareness.

Now, the sixth question Peggy came back with quickly. "What would you rather be experiencing?"

"I want to live. I want to do my part to improve our world. I want to have an amazing life with my wife and kids!"

Peggy moved forward with the seventh question. "What actions will you take to create what you'd rather be experiencing?"

Another easy answer for me. "Start working out, get checked out, and put a program in place."

And the final question in this series of questions was, "By when will you take those actions?"

That answer was easy. I promised, "Immediately!"

At this point, you'd think the exercise was over. In reality, it had only begun. Jack's instructions were pretty simple, "If you get done with one round of questions, go back through them again. You can expose a new issue, or you can delve deeper into the same issue that arose and start to *unpeel the onion,* as they say. You can go deeper and get to the source of these potentially limiting beliefs." That's exactly what we did. All my answers seemed to come out of the blue or at least I thought they did.

Now, it was round two. Peggy asked, "What's a disturbing or troubling situation in your life?"

I chose to explore my original answer further answering, "I'm fat."

Question two followed with, "How are you creating it or allowing it to happen?"

A little better understanding started to show up, "I haven't really acknowledged it fully, nor have I truly admitted that it is bothering me to the levels that it obviously is bothering me." The onion was shedding its layers.

This time question three started me down a whole other path. Peggy asked, "What are you pretending not to know?"

This time my answer was a whole lot more serious and targeted than simply, "I'm fat". I replied, "It's that by carrying all the extra weight and stressing myself to the levels I tend to stress myself, I could easily lose everything in my life that's important to me. I could lose my wife, my family, my career, and my ability to help others because I hadn't taken care of myself."

The fourth question was what opened up my realization for why I do what I do, "What is the payoff for keeping it this way?"

"It's easy". Again, this initial answer held true. But far more came out this time. This was the real shocker. I continued, "If I lose weight and become more fit, my wife may feel threatened that I am on the road all the time, speaking to so many people. And if I look better, someone might be interested in me." What? So, what if they did? Where did that come from? Was this ego talking? My relationship with my wife was awesome! Who did I think I was? She had never said anything like this, *ever*! We had an awesome and trusting marriage. Infidelity would never happen to either of us. We set that straight from the beginning.

This threw me for a total loop. Let me make sure you understand, my wife had never said anything like this to me. This was something that I totally manufactured in my mind. My wife, Peggy, has been my biggest supporter and ally through everything I have done. So then, why would I create something like this? On the one hand, I wish I knew. On the other hand, did it really matter? It was out in the open, so now it could be addressed and released.

Then question five came around the second time. The question was, "What is the cost for keeping it this way?" Because I had not taken responsibility for what I had been doing to myself, I had given away my power to food, fun, others, and you name it. The key here was that I thought I might in some way hurt my wife. This was something that I totally made up in my own mind. The true cost became sacrificing my long-term health for something that I only imagined existed. What an amazing realization!

Question six, the second time around, started the healing process. "What would you rather be experiencing?"

My answer was, "A fantastic and totally fulfilled life with an even happier and closer marriage. A long life of helping people achieve what they want to achieve and ultimately, making the contribution to humanity that I was put on this earth to provide."

The next question developed the initial action plan that was to be executed. The question was, "What actions will you take to create what you'd rather be experiencing?" The first answer came with absolutely no thought. In fact, it's amazing how your inner guidance will give you the right plan of attack if you let it.

Step one was to sit down with my wonderful wife Peggy, and discuss this entire exercise with her. I needed to fill her in on what had surfaced. Everything starting with the fact that the extra weight I carried was bothering me more than I ever knew and certainly let on to anyone. Then, I wanted to share that I had created this limiting belief about her concern, which she never actually had, and that I was committed to doing something about it.

Step two was to set up a time with Dr. Eisen for my CSANT scan. It was time to figure out what was going on with the chest pains I was having (but previously never had acknowledged).

Step three was simple. Start working out, eating properly, and doing what needed to be done.

We were making progress now. The final question in the series was, "By when will you take those actions?"

This answer was easy. "I have already started on fixing this! I've already changed the way that I am looking at all of this."

We still had time remaining for the exercise since answers were flowing freely. So, we began round three. It seemed as if the onion was down to its core. Oh no, it was not even close! The focus of this third round organically shifted to explore some of the existing answers in greater depth. It made complete sense to do this.

Here we go! Round three!

"What's a disturbing or troubling situation in your life?"

This answer took a little different turn. "That I do not feel like I can be fit on the road, because it would be a threat to my wife." Really? Did I believe that?

We went deeper. "How are you creating it or allowing it to happen?"

That was pretty obvious. "I totally manufactured this in my own mind. Peggy has never put anything like this on me. This is a total fabrication on my part. It's an excuse I created within my own psyche. And I'm using it to issue blame for something that I don't want to deal with."

This was getting really interesting and quite frankly, exposing things that I didn't know that I wanted to expose or that I even knew existed. The beauty of this exercise was its rapid-fire nature. Because of the bombardment of questions, it didn't give your brain much time to create an answer to the questions. It just kind of became your soul talking out loud.

The third question for the third time was, "What are you pretending not to know?"

Another answer came straight out of my gut. "That when I was in the best shape of my life, playing college football and later, when the Atkins diet did work for a short time, I really didn't like who I became." What? Huh? Did I really say that, too?

To say that this was a breakthrough is underestimating the value of what was taking place. The extra weight I was carrying was a shield, a figurative insulation layer that protected me and required me to be the person I wanted to be, to have people like me. It's hard to have a ton of ego flying around when you are out of shape.

The fourth question was asked. "What is the payoff for keeping it this way?" The realization came that there was very little if any payoff. It became evident that there was far more cost and it was potentially life-threatening. The next question followed.

"What is the cost for keeping it this way?" It was huge! I could not give it my all to do the things that have become very important to me. I wasn't at my very best and was limiting myself from living the best family life possible, having an incredible professional career and most importantly, creating the most positive impact possible to serve humanity.

"What would you rather be experiencing?"

"Everything I just mentioned to its fullest!"

"What actions will you take to create what you'd rather be experiencing?"

"The first thing I need to internalize is that I can be totally fit and be a great person at the same time. Second, that being fit, I can be an inspiration to so many others who are struggling with some of the same issues I've struggled with over my life. Third, that I will commit to an even greater level to serve and help others to achieve their highest vision. And finally, I will share what has happened in my life to hopefully inspire others that they too can regain control of their lives. They can do anything they desire to do and in doing so, become an inspiration to someone else. We can create a cyclone of positive impact to ultimately move our world forward."

"By when will you take those actions?"

"They have already started! This is exciting!"

I share this with you for many reasons. I had absolutely no idea any of this existed before we started this exercise. This shows the value of having mentors, people who have been there and done that before you. It also shows the value of constant and never-ending personal growth when it is a driving force in your life. You have so much to offer to so many. Doesn't it make sense to cultivate it and put it into action?

Awareness is having knowledge of the situations, opportunities, and consequences in all aspects of our lives. This eight-question exercise was amazingly powerful at bringing the necessary knowledge to the surface. Once revealed, an action plan could be created. Taking or retaking control of your life is where we go from here.

Another huge and new awareness that came to me through this process was that I had a number of hidden food allergies that I previously knew nothing about. Once I had the awareness that I truly wanted to get fit, I was referred to a nutritionist by a friend of mine, Dr. Fabrizio Mancini, the President Emeritus of Parker College of Chiropractic. One of the first things, JJ Virgin, my new nutritionist, had me do was a blood spot test which scanned for any food allergies. I never had any allergic reactions that I knew of. This brings to mind the old adage again, "You don't know what you don't know!"

What I didn't realize is that I had symptoms of food allergies for years, but never connected the dots. Or I should say, spots, as the case may be. Who would have thought sinus issues, bloating, gassiness, and fat retention were signs of allergies? Certainly not me! Boy, did I get a quick lesson and learn.

When my test results came back, I was found to be highly allergic to dairy, eggs, cheese, peanuts, cashews, almonds, and mildly allergic to mustard and pinto beans of all things. What? I grew up in Wisconsin. How could I be allergic to dairy? That's almost blasphemy!

The interesting thing to me as I read this list, was that all of the things I was allergic to, besides the pinto beans, were staples for me when I was on the Atkins diet. And this diet worked well for me! This and the fact that I grew up in Wisconsin living on dairy and cheese. Coincidence? I think not. Looking back, I had eaten so much of these foods, and almost exclusively during periods of my life, it seems reasonable to conclude I may have caused some of my own issues. What is important is that I found out and again could do something proactively to fix it.

While JJ could give you the expert's overview, let me give you a quick lay person's understanding of what happens with these food allergies. The body is designed to be perfect, so when we put something into it that it doesn't like or that it is "allergic" to, it creates antibodies to ward off the major effects. Our bodies do all they can to keep us from getting sick. It takes energy to produce these antibodies, and that energy comes from the breakdown of stored fat.

The body releases enough fat to produce the antibodies needed to combat this intrusion. The body also recognizes that if you eat this allergen once, you will probably do it again. As a result, it actually stores extra fat to ensure that the next time you eat the wrong food again, you won't get sick. Pretty ingenious! It's amazing how God created our bodies to work.

You have probably already identified the ensuing issue. You got it! You can work out for hours every day to try and lose weight like madmen or women, but to no avail. As long as you continue to put these allergens into your mouth, your body will release some, but not release all of your existing fat. Who knew? I didn't! The fat is there to protect you for the long run. Your body will hold only the right amount of fat based on your consumption and exertion. That's why if you don't know what you're allergic to, it becomes a vicious cycle. By the way, the good news is that the body will also learn to release excess stored fat once you have learned not to bombard it with allergens!

Awareness is truly the key to getting started. It is pretty hard to fix things you don't know about or are in denial over. Keeping an open mind and discarding any preconceived notions when it comes to fitness is very liberating. It allows you to address your individual situation and gives you the freedom to do something about it. Being perfectly created and open to the possibility that you can live the life of your dreams is tremendously exciting. Give yourself that opportunity. You deserve it!

Decide on Your Future

You have awakened! You've gained the awareness that things are not exactly as you would like them to be. Now it's time to take the next step toward your new life. The interesting part is, while most people believe that they truly know what they want out of life, very few people do. People tend to get caught up in life instead of purposefully designing it. That's really a shame, because we all have unlimited opportunity. Those who have taken advantage of those opportunities genuinely live a life of happiness and fulfillment.

To help you understand the importance of making a decision, let's revisit where the word comes from in the first place. It comes from the Latin word *decidere*, or *a cutting off or curtailment*. In its most literal sense, making a decision cuts off your old path and your old patterns. Your encouragement should be that you have done the best you could with what you have known up until today. Now, you know more, so you can do better! It comes down to your making a decision and taking the inspired actions that come from it.

Again Napoleon Hill wrote in his book, *Think and Grow Rich*, that one of the thirteen key characteristics to success is that you have to be decisive in nature. You have to make decisions. No decision is a decision. No action is an action. If you don't make a decision, someone will make it for you and you probably won't like the path it puts you on. Going with the flow may not necessarily be the best idea for you if you truly want to maximize your life's potential.

There are many reasons why people don't make decisions. In fact, the reasons or justifications for not making decisions would fill volumes. The point is, you have the opportunity to totally take control of *your* life. *You* can decide and design *your* future. And if you are in charge of designing it, doesn't it make sense to make it the very best it can possibly be?

To really take the first step toward your new life, you have to decide on your future. Sounds simple right? While fitness was high on my list of priorities, it has now become a means to an end. When I got down to looking at my life and where I really wanted it to go, quality of life really became the thing I was striving to achieve. And from the thousands of people I speak to around the world, that seems to be their number one goal in life as well—quality of life.

You cannot have quality of life if you are constantly fighting off demons from rearing their ugly heads at you in one particular area of your life. Quality of life comes through a great balance in all areas in our lives. Now, once I recognize a deficiency or an issue in a specific area of my life, I quickly take action to improve it. As I do this, many of the other demons pulling at me start to disappear. Identifying the issues, developing a plan of action, and working at the plan consistently has cured many ills.

Unfortunately, when it comes to making an improvement in a particular area, most people focus on the wrong thing. They focus on the negative situation they find themselves in versus the potential positive outcome. They focus on the negative aspects of being in debt. With money issues, it is not about being in debt, but becoming financially free. Huh? What do you mean?

If you want to get rid of debt, don't focus on reducing debt. You need to stop focusing on what you don't want, because whatever you focus on, you will get more of in your life. And you certainly don't want any more debt. If you really want to reduce debt, focus on financial freedom! By doing so, you will get the abundance you desire.

Think about it this way, whenever you lose anything, what's the first thing you do after you lose it? You work to find it! Regarding debt, what you lose and focus on, you tend to find again. This is the main reason bank account balances bounce up and down. You make progress for a short period of time, only to then incur more debt than ever. You continually jump back and forth. To truly achieve the results you desire for a lifetime, the decision you make has to be *life improvements* and *positive financial improvements* at that.

As you are deciding on your future, doesn't it make sense to have it be everything you could have it become? With that being the case, we can achieve any level of wealth that any other comparable person in the world has accomplished. All we have to do is understand what they've done, how they did it, and do the same thing.

When you know the ingredients necessary to be wealthy, and execute the recipe that combines them all, you will achieve the same results. That's all I did. I found out what wealthy people did to become and stay financially free and did the same things. This is not rocket science! It's also another reason for writing this book—to share with you what I have learned as a person who has been there and done that. The goal is for you to be able to live a greater, more prosperous, higher quality, and longer life.

Throughout history, great thinkers, and the super successful have always thought way ahead of where they were at that particular time. Steven Covey, in his book, *7 Habits of Highly Effective People* states, "You have to begin with the end in mind!" Tony Robbins, one of the greatest motivational speakers of our time, describes it this way, "You have to know your outcome." Jack Canfield, America's Success Coach and co-author of the *Chicken Soup for the Soul*® series says, "You have to start with a vision." All three of these unbelievable trainers, authors, and motivators all start from the same place. It's not where you are today that determines your outcomes in life, it's ultimately where you want to go and how vividly you can picture that place within your mind. Henry Ford said it many years ago. "Think you can, think you can't, you're right either way!"

Your decision sets everything in motion. We live in an abundant universe. Everything you need to be successful is available, once you know what you want. Your mind will lead you to what you need to focus on next. If your desire is to become financially free or wealthy, find a picture of what financial freedom looks like to you. Then, tape it up on a surface you look at consistently. Meditate on what you want to look like being financially free. This visual will guide you on that path.

We all have an inner guidance system. Again, we are all designed as perfect beings. Your inner guidance works much like the Global Positioning System or GPS in your vehicle. A GPS is an amazing piece of technology. It uses twenty-four satellites that are in geo-synchronous orbit or distributed equally around the earth in a constant orbit. The GPS system signals the satellites and by triangulating the signals from the closest three satellites, it can tell you exactly where you are. Its accuracy is within a few feet. As soon as you put in your destination, it automatically calculates the route you can take, to get from where you are, to where you want to be. In fact, it will even give you alternative routes if you desire.

Hopefully, you are getting the analogy. When you know the destination of where you want to go, finding the route to getting there is easy. You can even have multiple routes. The key is, you need to know where you want to go. Just as a GPS cannot give guidance until you program it, your inner guidance works the same way. As soon as you give it the destination, you're off and running.

Most people tend to work hard to program their inner guidance to go to all the places they don't really want to go. The inner guidance's only task is to guide you to where you say you want to go. It knows where to deliver you, so if you continually fill it with bad information, guess where it takes you? Get in touch with what you really want. Then, program your inner guidance to take you there, so you can truly achieve success.

I even created an affirmation to consistently remind me. It was, "I'm happy as can be, being financially free!" (See page 143 for more affirmations for your review and usage). My inner GPS now had an achievable destination to head for.

There are many people who can help you figure out the right targets for you. If the desire is to be financially free, the focus is on financial freedom. Do what wealthy people do, invest like wealthy people invest, and study what wealthy people study.

The bottom line is that you have to want it! This has to be your decision and your commitment. As Jim Rohn says, "You can't hire anyone else to do your push-ups for you!" You have to become financially free because *you* want to become financially free, not for anyone or anything else. For me, I realized that I could not accomplish the many things in my life that were important to me if I remained on the financial path I was on.

When you step back and take a look at what's really important in your life, this becomes a very simple decision. Don't believe me? Let's take a closer look. Are you married or have a significant other? How does that future look if you are out of the picture, either by restricted ability or just not there? Do you have kids? How do they get the best that you have to offer? Professionally, are there some great things you want to accomplish? How do they come to fruition without your leading the way? Spiritually, are you achieving the levels that your higher source has put you here to achieve?

I think you probably get the idea. Again, none of this has anything to do with anybody else's path for your life. This all has to do with who *you* are and what *you* want to accomplish. There is also no judgment or critique here. I lived for 61 years of my life believing that I was happy, healthy, and on a successful path. It wasn't until I decided that an already great life could be better, if I chose to do something more. What I found out is that you truly "don't know what you don't know" until you find it out.

You can be anything you want to be and have all that you want to have in this life. And there is one thing for certain. Nobody can make you do something that you don't want to do to be successful in the long run. Have you ever had someone tell you not to take an action or heavily suggest you have to do something else? Simply put, it's a pain. It's no fun for you and probably even less fun for them. When you make the decisions, you call the shots. Now, that's fun!

For me, the decision was simple. I wanted the best quality of life that I could have personally, professionally, and spiritually. In looking at how that could be achieved, the answer became obvious. The answer to achieving greater fulfillment across all three of these areas of my life was getting fit! We all have the same opportunities in life. The difference is that those who take advantage of those opportunities are usually called successful. Is that what you really want? You can have it! You can have it now! You just have to decide on your future!

Redesign Your Activities

It's time to get after it. Einstein stated many years ago, "The level of thinking that created your problem is not the same level of thinking required to solve it." In fact, he stated his definition of insanity as "doing the same things, the same way, and expecting different results." If you want to achieve a whole new level in any area of your life or experience the byproducts that come along with it, you have to redesign your activities. You have to make some changes or better yet, some improvements in your life.

Understand right out of the blocks, after you make this decision to take control of your life, this may or may not be a popular decision with those around you. Am I saying that some of the people around you who truly love and care for you won't like the decision you make to improve? That's exactly what I'm saying. It's not out of spite, and it's not out of malice. It's because they are human. People naturally love to improve, but they hate to change. Unfortunately, in this day and age, there is nothing as constant as change. The net result is that sometimes as you cast your change upon them, they may resist. Embrace their resistance just like you will embrace many other things along the way. Understand that many times it is just part of the process.

Initially, most people will rally around you, giving you encouragement, and supporting you on your path. Beware, as this can be short-lived. They love you, want the best for you, but they are not *you*! There is only one you and that's *you*! To be truly successful on your path, you need to be doing this for *you* first. The drive has to be within you, because there will be times that everyone else will say, "You've done great....Now, enough is enough!...Let's go grab *whatever*. You've done so well, it's okay to regress a little bit, right?" It's tempting, really tempting, but you are doing this for a greater purpose, which is your overall well-being!

Before we move on, let's address the last statement about friends encouraging you to deviate from your plans. I grew up on pizza and beer, all the way to 256 pounds. Bottom line, doing certain things that successful people don't do are not what successful people do. It's not for us to question why, it's just the facts! It's not that you can't do certain things. Remember, you are totally responsible for you. It really becomes more about why you would want to? You are making such great progress daily, so why would you want to hinder your fantastic results?

There are going to be some things that you used to do that you will realize you don't want to do going forward. They're not evil, they're not treacherous, but they are not done by people with a desire to have spectacular results for the rest of their lives. Again, it's not about focusing on giving some things up. It's focusing on the overall quality of life you will experience for the rest of your days.

As you redesign your activities, you are going to have to do a critical review of what you already do in your life. And you have to be brutally honest. If you truly want to change, you need to totally understand the baseline you are starting from. It is what it is, and you are where you are. The exciting part is that you are committed to do something about it.

You have an advantage. You're already living in the real world. So, for you, you can redesign your activities based on your life as it is today. Please don't use where you are today, or everything you have to do, to make excuses. They are things to be reviewed and modified in a way that is consistent with the new and improved you. Keep visualizing a picture of yourself as you want to be.

We live in a society which seeks immediate gratification. It's hard to look past where we are at the moment to truly understand where we could be in the future, whether this is positive or negative. What I came to realize is, that if I continued the path I was on, there wouldn't be much of a future. And that was not very exciting to me in the least! I'm not just talking about death here. I'm really talking about living a life that is nowhere near the quality that it could be. That's flat out a waste of what we were put on earth to experience. You and those you love have so much God-given potential. It is really a shame that most people don't maximize their lives. I certainly didn't for many years.

We have all been blessed in so many ways. Why is it that we don't seem to treasure it the way we should? As a friend of mine has said to me many times, "Yesterday is history, tomorrow's a mystery, and today is a gift. That's why they call it the present!" We can make every day special in every way if we choose to. It's up to you individually. That's why you have to be honest with yourself. You know what you are doing or not doing. You know what actions you are taking and those you are not taking. This is important, because you are worth it!

So, how do you go about redesigning your activities? Simple! You first have to get a handle on what's happening with you now. Every day log your activities—period! If it goes through your lips, you write it down. If you go buy a Starbucks, you write it down. If you have greater success professionally, you write it down. It's the only way that you will truly track your activities and know them.

In a recent conversation with a friend, we were discussing this idea and he gave a great example through a conversation he had with his son. His son had a $1,000/month expense budget and his only responsibilities were for the groceries, his monthly phone bill, and the gas he put in his car. Should be no problem, right? Every month, he ran out of money. He had no idea why. After his dad suggested documenting everything he spent his money on, he came to an astonishing conclusion. He was spending about $350/month at Starbucks! That's a car payment or some other payment that could have made his life easier and better.

We tend to not realize exactly how much we consume, spend, socialize, or waste time. It's not on purpose. It just happens. The systems we put in place are necessary to live our lives to the fullest. This is a mindset we all can achieve.

Let me warn you, as you start to journal, you probably will not like what you see, but it is an eye opener. It certainly was for me! You never realize exactly how much stuff you are consuming beyond what you really like or need. It's actually very educational.

If you can manage logging your activities similarly, you'll be way ahead. This may sound like a daunting task, but in fact, it's really pretty easy. If you haven't guessed it already, measurability of any and everything becomes really important. You get the idea?

Here's the bottom line, you would not be reading this book unless either you personally had a desire to improve your life or you wanted to share these concepts with those you love to help them improve their lives. In either case, you have to have an open mind to what may be new to you to create the desired results going forward. Much of this was a smack upside my head and my response was, "Thank you, sir! May I have another!" Sometimes a gentle nudge is what we all need to gain the awareness necessary to move forward.

These tools are life-saving and enhancement devices. When you use them, your life is better for it. The question becomes, are you serious and committed enough to do what it takes to take care of yourself *first?* The potential inconveniences are minor in comparison to the benefits you will receive by using these tools *consistently.*

This final part of redesigning your activities may seem unique. It is much like what someone would go through recovering from some type of addiction. In heading into your new life, you must learn to develop feelings, thoughts and behaviors that support your new found improvements. These must replace the ones you had prior to gaining ground on your previous issues.

You need to understand addiction and the overall effects addictive behavior has on what is going on in your life. Learning to identify skills that allow you to cope with the newness of what you will be going through, and learning to refuse the activities you choose not to participate in, will be important. The key to your success will include creating a support system based on a more productive lifestyle. You'll be amazed at how your self-worth and self-esteem will skyrocket. And your desire to contribute to others' success will grow. Your passion for life will expand.

This is also going to be a time of self-examination to make sure you are staying the course. Stay committed to your new habits and don't fall into self-sabotage with your old habits. Redesigning your activities will play a huge part in your ongoing success for the rest of your life. No matter where you are in your life today, you can make the changes necessary to live a happier and more fulfilling life.

Execute the Plan

I bet there are a number of you at this point chomping at the bit. You can't wait to get started and just want the plan you need to put into action. All right, you'll get that full plan here soon. It's important going into this to understand all the steps of *A Dream I Live* to ensure ongoing success. Had we jumped into the rest of the plan before awakening your awareness, deciding on your future, and redesigning your activities, the chances are you would not maintain the plan over an extended period of time. As they say, patience is a virtue.

Executing the plan becomes the cornerstone of your lifelong success. This is your starting point to the rest of your life. Over time, as you develop and your quality of life increases, this plan will change and need to be modified. But again, you still have to have a starting point.

The first part of the *A Dream I Live* plan takes very little explanation. Here it is: Read the Bible or the spiritual material of your choosing, a minimum of 30 minutes per day and five days per week. But Scott, what are you saying? You don't understand my schedule. Yes, I do. I had the same schedule or a potentially worse one. You have to commit to make it happen and then train yourself to do it. This is important. It may take a few weeks, but as soon as you hit your stride, you will feel the difference spiritually immediately.

Professionally, commit to reading or studying articles or books on how to do your job better and improve your interactions with other business professionals. Stephen Covey, in *7 Habits of Highly Effective People* said, "You have to sharpen the saw!" Learn the skills, understand the workflow, and learn the things that make the greatest from your industry great!

Physically, get your move on. Walk 30 minutes a day. Jog two miles and take at least one yoga class each week. Do the physical activities that get you to the level of fitness you desire.

Financially, put a savings program into place. Go to a seminar and gain knowledge on how to trade your own money in the stock market. Learn how to write covered calls, and execute one trade a month that typically averages four to nine percent *each* month. Get a financial mentor.

Socially, re-engage with friends you may have lost track of. Reach out to those you enjoy spending time with, and actually go and spend time together. Reach out to old friends via social media. Make old friends your new friends by catching up on what's happened since you last interacted. Play Contact List Roulette (page 129).

When it comes to giving back, contribute! The most precious resource that any of us have is our time. Volunteer if and when you can. Make the effort to get actively involved. Spending time with someone else provides an amazing investment for both of you. If you can donate money to forward a cause, donate. Whatever you can do to make a positive impact, do it!

And finally, do something for yourself. This is your personal side. A little self-care and nurturing are called for, because you deserve it. The word recreation can actually be spelled re-creation. Re-create a fresh, new, and enthused you by finding something that recharges your batteries, and gets you ready to take on the world once again.

What it comes down to, is having a plan and putting it into action. The only way you know if this will work for you and help you achieve the results you truly desire is by taking action.

There is no shortage of ideas, ways to have fun, or places to see around the country to refresh you. These are ultimately investments in the best product you can invest in—*you*!

Analyze the Results

You have been executing the plan to perfection. How do you know everything is working out the way you want it to? Like any goal, measurability becomes very important. You have to be able to determine *how much, by when*. It's what keeps you going and on track. The critical ingredient is recording a variety of measurements before you start on your journey. You have to create a baseline of where you are at the moment.

In each area of life, the measurables may vary. Are you moving closer to or further from your goals? Is your bank account growing or receding? Are you getting physically stronger or weaker? Are you spending more or less time with those you love? The only way to truly understand your growth is to have benchmarks with defined time frames.

How specific those benchmarks are or how rigid they may be is up to you. At this stage, you have to analyze and evaluate your progress. As my friend, Dean Lindsay, says in his book *The Progress Agent*, "All progress is change, but not all change is progress!"

The likelihood of everything you initially put into action as being the perfect answer for you and your situation, is slim to none. In going from where you are, to where you want to be, you are going to have to adapt. Anytime we do anything consistently (about six weeks), our bodies and minds learn to accept it as the norm. That means, by definition, we are going to have to modify our plans and re-execute accordingly.

What needs to happen first is for you to take the input you receive to *Analyze the Results*. Evaluate the results and critically look for alternatives that will take you on a more direct route to your goals. This may be better conveyed through a story I use in my training programs.

When a plane is ready to fly from Dallas to Honolulu, the pilots establish a flight plan that charts out exactly how they want to get from point A to point B. They have every intention of following that plan to the T. The challenge is that as soon as they lift off the ground, there are outside forces that start to come into play. It may be the jet stream, it could be weather patterns, and it might even be other aircraft trying to fly in the same airspace. Regardless of the obstacle, the pilots know where they need to get to. To assure they arrive at their desired destination, they are constantly correcting their course to achieve the end result. That is, to land in Honolulu.

They would never come on the PA or public address system and say something like, "Sorry, ladies and gentlemen. I know you probably had your heart set on a great vacation in Hawaii. But, because of some significantly heavy southerly trade winds, you'll now be enjoying a stay in Alaska!" That would never happen. That's ridiculous. Of course it is! But it is no more ridiculous to set out with a longing to live a fulfilling life and settling for being moderately happy instead. Or, being financially free versus living paycheck to paycheck.

Life is a journey, not a destination. If you want to be fit, you can be fit. If you want abundance, you can have abundance. Sometimes, you might get a little off course. The good news is, unlike the pilots who are off course far more than they are on course, your adjustments and modifications hopefully do not have to be as dramatic or happen as often.

Understand that you will be off course a fair amount of the time. Getting off course is not the issue. *Staying* off course is the issue. As soon as you recognize it, get back to doing what you should be doing. This kind of discipline takes place one day at a time. So, how do you determine what needs to be done to get you back on course?

It's actually pretty simple. Ask yourself these questions with regard to each of the seven critical and non-negotiable areas of life—spiritual, professional, financial, health, social relationships, contributions, and your personal life. What's working? What's not working? What could be better? What could you do to make it better?

Modify the Plan & Re-Execute

In a seminar setting, we used to do a feedback exercise. We would blindfold a participant, spin them around gently, and then ask them to walk across the room while being guided by the sound of another person's voice. Without question, at some point, the participant would take too many steps to the right or left. The person leading them would immediately say, "Off course!" Then, they would course correct them with the command, "On course".

This is an example of modifying the plan and re-executing it immediately. Throughout the course of your life, things are going to come up. People will work to influence or even sabotage you. If you keep your eyes open, this will be an amazing learning experience, because each day is a totally new day.

Any time you are making modifications in your life, be aware that not everyone always wants you to make those modifications. The first lesson I learned when I made some major improvements in my life was that unfortunately, numerous people were looking to find a negative, rather than a positive result with my progress. It opened my eyes to the fact that we all need to be encouragers of others and not vision vandals.

There is a gift in this process regardless. The gift is that there are people who genuinely care about you and your well-being. Be sure to recognize this, even when there are a few who are not rooting for you. People who I didn't really think even knew me, cared about me. It was a great feeling to feel that love and concern from so many people. Now I was even more encouraged.

What did I do to create this gift? I created it by sharing publicly, the improvements I wanted to make, so people could see the results. More importantly, I could make modifications by talking more to people about my reasons for doing what I'm doing, and hopefully encourage them to take similar action.

This is actually one of the driving forces for writing this book. This book becomes an accountability piece for me going forward. How can I give others a step-by-step plan on how to retake control of their lives? I never anticipated writing a book on the seven areas of life when I began to get to work on my own life.

After observing what I have done, people consistently come up to me asking if I would share it with them. It became apparent that I needed to modify my plan and take the time to write this book.

Persistence and perseverance are key to all of this. The chances of gaining a perfect result with everything you execute is highly unlikely. A great friend and mentor of mine, Dr. John Dealey, reminded me of this from time to time when I lost patience with my progress in some areas of life. If you strive for a one percent increase each day, by the end of the year, you'll have a 365 percent increase. Anybody would love to have that kind of growth year over year.

On course or off course are directions to be recognized. If you are on course, work diligently to stay the course. And if you are off course, you deserve acknowledgment for recognizing it. Now, get back to what you originally intended. Pretty simple, huh?

There are times when we execute the plan and no matter what we seem to do with the very best intentions, we don't achieve the desired results. This is a time when you may want to look even deeper into your past to identify and release some of the potentially limiting beliefs you have developed over your lifetime. This was very powerful to me when I learned about it. It made great sense to explore all the methods and techniques available to live the life I dreamed of.

There are some other modifications that can take place if you are open to what could be a totally new and expanding world. What I'm talking about is the world of release techniques. Throughout our lifetime, we have had a myriad of things placed on us, said to us, done to us, etc. Many times, we have no clear recollection that these things ever transpired. They may have happened when we were very young. Perhaps they were very painful experiences we blocked out of our recallable memories. The fact is things happened to all of us and they shaped who we are today. The good, the bad, and the ugly.

My personal belief is that if you truly want to maximize the quality of your life and the lives of those you love around you, it is imperative that you explore some release techniques. If you've never heard of this concept before, that's okay. You've heard about it now. Here's another way of looking at it. If you grew up and have been able to make it to where you are today with absolutely no issues in the back of your mind, no limiting beliefs, and no *bad tapes* playing in your head, congratulations! You will fly through the release process.

But, if you do have hidden *junk in your trunk*, you will be forever grateful that you learned how to identify your junk, forgive, and move forward for the rest of your life. Let's look at being overweight, as our example. The chances are that if you are not fit, and you are overweight, there is someone or some reason that is causing your situation. The obvious causes are that you consume too much, sleep too little, and barely exercise. Even these three things are more like symptoms, than root causes.

If you don't feel loved or appreciated, it's easy to turn to food as a comfort item. If you heard your dad tell your mom her arms looked big, and that hurt her feelings, you may never want to gain muscle mass, because you feel you might hear something similar. Throughout our lives, there are many misinterpretations that we create and apply to incidents in our lives. These misinterpretations left unchecked or at least unexplored, can really hold you back from enjoying your best life possible.

There are a number of ways to address these past issues. Fortunately, there have been many healers I've crossed paths with throughout my life. Let me share with you three of the best. The first is Dr. John DeVore. John is a chiropractor who has an absolute gift as an intuitive healer. Throughout his chiropractic career, he has continued to educate himself with the best of the best. John went on to incorporate a number of healing modalities into one process he named The DeVore Method.

I have been blessed to be treated by Dr. DeVore many times. During each treatment, we uncover and release another deep-seated issue that had the potential to hold me back from living my best life. This process has been like unpeeling an onion. Once released, you move progressively closer to your desired outcomes and a greater life experience.

To understand the DeVore Method, you first have to realize what gets in the way of abundant living and receiving all we are meant to receive. There are resistant thoughts that have developed over time. When we're born, there is no rule book to learn from and follow. We develop our responses and actions based on what we learn through our environments, families, and life situations. In other words, we create files within our minds to store these experiences as a way to provide ongoing guidance in the future. The challenge comes in that not every piece of information in these files is positive or helpful.

The body and brain have been perfectly produced to hold these files and call upon them throughout our lives. The next challenge is that not every file allows you to move toward the desired outcome you want. Many times, these files need to be updated years after they were originally created. The potential problem with a new set of instructions is that the file is already full. So naturally, we resist or create blocks to the new instructions. These blocks lead to your inability to address certain issues or change certain things even when you really, really want to. Hence, the reason for working with an expert like Dr. DeVore to release the bad files that hold you back from achieving a higher level of fulfillment.

The bottom line to what Dr. DeVore does is to release things from the past that keep you from moving forward today. It's quick, painless, and from personal experience, makes a huge difference going forward.

The second great healer I have had the pleasure to get to know is Hale Dwoskin. Hale runs Sedona Training Associates, which was founded in 1966, to promote the revolutionary discoveries of Hale's mentor and friend, physicist, and engineer, Lester Levenson. Sedona, Arizona is the home of The Sedona Method. This method is a release technique that once learned, can be done anytime, anywhere, by anyone. It is used to address everything from immediate aches and pains, to lifelong issues that have been impairing you. When I first met Hale, I was in absolute awe of what he could accomplish to help me and others in such a short period of time and with so little effort.

The Sedona Method is a powerful and easy-to-learn technique that allows you to use your natural ability to let go of painful or unwanted feelings in that moment. It consists of a series of questions you ask yourself that leads your awareness to what you are feeling in the moment. You are then gently guided into the experience of letting it go. It's amazing how simple it is to learn this technique. More importantly, the results speak for themselves.

Using The Sedona Method, you can experience dramatic shifts in self-esteem, self-confidence, freedom from fear or anxiety, depression, emotional traumas, and more. It has been proven to be effective with a number of habitual and self-defeating behaviors including overeating, drinking, and smoking; none of which are characteristics or activities of fit and healthy people.

The Sedona Method is based on the power of feelings. When you feel powerful, you act powerfully. When you feel sad, you act sadly. Your feelings define how you operate in the world. And, unless you change those feelings, you are going to act as you have always acted and produce the results you have always produced. If you are stuck in your striving for improvement, The Sedona Method could be the key that unlocks your success.

Hale's book on this subject is entitled *The Sedona Method,* and he can be reached at *www.sedona.com*. This is another great way to improve your results no matter where you started.

One additional release technique worth your exploration is the Emotional Freedom Technique. Fellow Platinum Masterminder, Martin Lishcolnig, from Austria is an expert in the Emotional Freedom Technique (EFT). This is a technique that again can be used anywhere, at anytime to eliminate virtually any ache, pain, or deep-set issue that may be plaguing you.

EFT is an emotional, needle-free version of acupuncture that is based on new discoveries regarding the connection between your body's subtle energies, your emotions, and your health. EFT is extremely easy to execute, and anyone can take advantage of it once they learn how. EFT is executed by using your fingertips and a process of tapping certain meridian points to stimulate them. Unbalanced energy meridians can be a cause for emotional stress which contributes to pain, disease, and physical ailments.

The easiest way to see if you would benefit from EFT is to give it a try. You can learn more by going to *www.emofree.com*. No matter which method or guru you choose to follow, you can only benefit from being exposed to these release techniques. Personally, I have used them all and experienced great results. Living closest to Dr. DeVore and being able to take advantage of his expertise one-on-one more easily, I've found his DeVore Method to be exceptional. Every time he has treated me, there have been immediate positive results. After all, that is what you're looking for, right?

In essence, forward movement in your life comes down to *persistence, perseverance, and patience.* To truly be successful over the long haul, you are going to have to modify your approach and get after it again. The good news is, it will pay off and you will feel fabulous for it. The exciting part is that this is your life, and you deserve to make it everything you want and more. It also means that you can go from where you are now, to where you want to be in a matter of days, weeks, or even months. You will achieve your dreams and desires when you stay in action.

Inspire Others

Inspiration is the *stimulation of the mind or emotions to a high level of feeling or activity.* Being in the spirit and being right with your higher source, as well as everything and everyone that higher source has created, is essential. It is born and bred within your soul and comes out allowing you to serve the greater good.

Congratulations on your continued path to greater happiness and a more fulfilled life! Are you feeling better about the path ahead of you? How about your ability to achieve the desired results? With all my heart, I truly hope so. If you are not quite there yet, meaning you still have some doubt, go back and reread the book.

Accompanying this book is also an excellent, exciting 112-page, *Pause and Ponder Action Journal* which is filled with additional exercises, techniques, tips and plans to explore and solidify your new thoughts, directions, life choices, and results. The journal can be obtained @ http://TSWNbook.com.

Take some time to absorb the information contained in this book and journal. They are laid out in a way that lets anyone execute all of the ideas, workouts, and plans if they truly want to. Use these resources to your advantage.

One of the things I have learned through this experience of improving my life is what an inspiration I have been to so many. This wasn't necessarily the motivation behind why I did it, but after hearing dozens of thanks from so many different people, many I have never met before, I decided I had to share these concepts. We really have no idea exactly how many people are observing our every move, and who we will impact positively.

As I just mentioned, many times we are watched by people and can be caught doing something wrong. Or, there could be misconceptions which cause people to see us negatively. Maybe some people feel that by catching us not walking the talk, this will elevate them and make them feel better about themselves. Oddly enough, that might even provide them with some inspiration.

There is a huge difference between inspiration and motivation. To me, inspiration is so much more powerful and far longer-lasting because it is an internally driven force. Inspiration comes from within you individually. It is an inside-out activity. When others receive inspiration from what you are doing or have accomplished, they have started their own fires burning internally which will ultimately keep going long after your interaction with them is finished. They now have a natural enthusiasm for what they are doing. Remember, enthusiasm comes from the Greek, *En Theos*, or *of God's Spirit*. Inspiration and enthusiasm go hand in hand.

Motivation has an outside-in orientation. It typically comes from someone or something else as they motivate you to do something you probably don't want to do in the first place. The problem is simple here. Once that person or thing is gone, so is the motivation. To truly keep going for the rest of your life, you need to internalize the *why* you want to do this. You need to catch the spirit and be enthused about the possibilities.

It seems much better when we make a purposeful attempt to provide that positive inspiration. Throughout my life, I have been very blessed to work with so many wonderful mentors and teachers. They have shared their insights, wisdom, knowledge, and friendship with me along the way. Each and every one of them has been an inspiration to me in my personal growth. The commitment made in return to each one of them was the same. I would take what I had learned, add to it the experiences I gained from executing what I learned, and pay it forward to others.

It's really about finding a higher purpose for your life rather than simply living life. I truly believe we have been put on this earth for a couple of reasons. First off is to have a fabulous life. And secondly, to help as many people as we can. It's extremely obvious that if you are not having a fabulous life, you are missing the first and most important part of this equation.

You can have a good life without working to constantly improve, but I'm not sure if it can be a great life. This is not a judgment, but just an observation. As much as anything, I am speaking from personal experience. You owe it to yourself and those you love around you to be the best you that you can be. When you don't take care of yourself, you usually do not have all the capabilities you could have available to help someone else.

A big part of inspiring others is to first inspire you. Have a higher purpose in life and really get outside yourself. Here's an example of what I mean by that. When I started working out frequently, especially when lifting weights, I'd really wanted to quit! I was ready to give up, stop, and hasta la bye-bye. I felt totally uninspired and unmotivated. Not continuing or pushing through was not an option in the grand scheme of things. So, what do you do? Get outside yourself! I created a mental image that would provide me with that inspiration when I needed to draw upon it. It's pretty simple. Read the next paragraph and see if you can put yourself in that same place.

Have you ever seen the Verizon Wireless commercials that show the representatives of the Verizon network? You know the ones that show all the Verizon people there to support your every need when you go to make a call? Because these commercials are on virtually every channel a gazillion times a day, I had a very vivid picture in my mind of all those people standing in front of me. The thought came to me to use this practice of having a picture or mental image to provide what I needed to take action when I didn't want to.

I simply reassigned the reason for placing those people in that commercial. In my mind, that gaggle of Verizon people depicted all the people depending upon me for inspiration going forward. I imagined they depended on me not only for what I was working on, but also in regard to the topics I speak about as well. Immediately, I felt a responsibility to them and had no desire to let them down by not being my best self. That image in my mind provides me the inspiration I need when I don't feel it! It's a neat little mental trick.

Another part of providing inspiration is living your message. You have to be full of integrity, and I wasn't! A number of years ago, when I made the decision to right size my body, my words were not congruent with my physical actions. To understand this better is to understand these following communication concepts. Only seven percent of your communication is words. Thirty-eight percent is from your tonality, inflection, and the pacing in which it is delivered. And fifty-five percent is the physiology. Physiology includes gesturing, movements, and posture. It also includes your physical appearance. *You are the message!*

As a speaker who works to help others achieve their highest vision, it was totally inconsistent to share the message of achieving more, taking control of your life, and reaching your highest potential while visibly, I was so out of shape myself. The worst part was that I never even realized it. It's not like anyone ever came up to me and said, "Hey, nice talk about taking control of your life—Fatty!"

As weird as it may sound, I almost wish they had. Maybe it would have alerted me to the issues and possibilities sooner. In thinking about it, God's timing is perfect. So, it all happened exactly the way it was supposed to happen. The point is that more messages are being heard, internalized, and accepted by the audiences I speak to today.

The messages are more effective because the delivery vehicle, which is me, is better. There are probably additional reasons for this including higher self-esteem, greater confidence, and better energy, now that I have a greater level of fitness. It's amazing how many positive attributes you become aware of once you gain your fitness back.

This is another one of those situations in life when you "don't know what you don't know!" Before you become fit, you probably feel like everything is okay. It's not until after you make the changes that you really feel and see the differences. Again, from personal experience, you are going to love the way you feel!

Creating and living your legacy is a way of providing inspiration to others. We all have so much that we can do for others, it just makes plain sense. Everyone knows someone who absolutely inspires them to do more. Who did you just think of? Somebody popped into your mind, didn't they? Who is the person you want to emulate, and grow up to be like? Who do you generally admire for what they have been able to accomplish in life? The fact of the matter is that we are all going to leave a legacy when we pass. The better question is, what will that legacy look like? Is it positive? Will people want to follow your lead? Or vow to be nothing like you?

We all have capabilities far beyond what we use on a consistent basis. With that, we all have the ability to provide value to other human beings on this planet. Everyone knows at least one thing that someone else doesn't know but needs to know. If you think about it, it's really not that hard to be an inspiration to someone else. It just takes a little thought and desire.

One of my favorite teachers on the concept of inspiration was Wayne Dyer. He had an amazing ability to take a complex subject, like inspiration, and make it so easy to understand. In a recent presentation aired for PBS on inspiration, he talked about the benefits of being inspired. Here's the way he put it, along with my takeaways from what he said.

When you are inspired: 1) your thoughts break their bonds. To me, that's a great way to say that we become far more creative and let our inner genius come out and play. 2) your mind transcends limitations. We finally access the excess capacity we all have in our brains to think outside-the-box. 3) your consciousness expands in every direction; You really start to get outside yourself and realize there is far more to life than just your little world. 4) you find yourself in a new, great, and wonderful world! My gut says you become far more grateful for everything you have as opposed to searching for what you don't have. It is the realization that no matter what, life is good! 5) your dormant focus, faculties, and talents come alive! This is when you become the best you that you can be and truly live the life of your dreams. 6) you discover yourself to be a greater person than you ever dreamed yourself to be! This is when you realize that you are enough!

You are an amazing being with so much potential to make a positive impact in this world. That's hugely exciting!

Dr. Dyer went on to say that when you are inspired in spirit, and you announce your desires that are aligned with your purpose, you are on your way! It is very comforting for me to live inspired. There is a natural enthusiasm and zest for life that comes with it.

Hopefully, you feel a certain desire to inspire others to be the best they can be. It is a natural instinct that far too often gets squashed by our environment and today's torrid pace. If you slow down for just a few minutes and think about what is really important in your life, I think you will find that internal inspiration when tapped, will allow you to live a remarkable and far more fulfilling life.

Chapter 8

ACTION PLAN FOR LIVING ON PURPOSE

LIVE on Purpose

LIVE is an acronym to help you remember more of what life is all about. Speaking again from personal experience, these areas have been moved aside from time to time due to the pressures of everyday life. It's nothing to be proud of, nor is it an excuse to keep it that way. To a certain extent, creating this acronym is almost an epiphany. Each and every one of us can live the life of our dreams. It doesn't need to be a struggle. It doesn't need to be difficult, and it doesn't need to be the same old, same old. You can have what you want. As Napoleon Hill said, "Whatever man can conceive and believe, he can achieve!"

How does this concept belong in a book about living your legacy? It's pretty simple actually. As you reach your significance goals, you will find yourself far more in tune with your body, mind, and spirit. You will achieve a greater calm and optimism than you have ever encountered previously. I wish I knew exactly why this is true. You just have to take my word for it. At the very least, isn't this worth striving for? This is more the philosophical approach. It comes from at least one man's real-world experience, mine!

LOVE

The "L" in LIVE stands for love. The first person you need to love, is yourself. You are absolutely amazing in every way! Sure, maybe some things have gotten out of whack. Stuff happens! The great news is that you have recognized it and are committed to doing something positive about it. Don't be so hard on yourself. Give yourself permission to love yourself. Most people are their own worst inner critic. If that's you, get over it. If you take a minute and really think about it, you have accomplished some amazing things throughout your life!

Recently, for a Mastermind presentation, my homework was to look back over my life in nineteen-year increments, (ages 0 to 19, 20 to 39, 40 to 59, etc.). I was to detail at least three significant events or accomplishments during that period of time. It was fascinating! After completing the exercise, it became very evident that I had many monumental achievements. The best part was that I hadn't thought of these events for years. To be able to go back, relive them, and experience the positive feelings associated with them was amazing.

Here's the net result of this type of exercise—you are enough! You have done many things that you should be proud of in so many ways. And once you reestablish that gratitude for what you have already accomplished, you will create the internal inspiration necessary to do whatever it is in life that you want to do.

The next group that you need to share your love with is your family. Sometimes that's easy, sometimes not so much, and sometimes it seems impossible. No matter what your experiences have been with family, they have helped craft who you have become—the good, the bad, and the ugly.

It seems family or at least your perception of family has a tendency to change with time—that sibling who made your life a nightmare, or who was your biggest supporter, helped shape who you have become. Parents have provided a model for whatever you decided to become or rebel against. Again, either way, family has shaped who you are. Be grateful for all you experienced.

And finally, love your friends. Life would be a lonely place without friends. Sometimes friendships seem like a lot of work, while other times they are as easy as it gets. Again, there are blessings in either case. Value those who have befriended you along the way. Thank them for their contributions to who you've become.

INVEST

The "I" in LIVE stands for invest. It only makes sense that we individually invest in ourselves as well as in humanity itself. Here's the bottom line folks. We're all in this together. The interesting part is that you control whether you believe this or not. It's really easy in today's fast-paced, dog-eat-dog world, to grasp for a Darwinian ideal of the survival of the fittest. Sure, you can adopt this belief and you can climb to the top, but the other 7.4 billion people on this planet are still going to be here.

It seems to make more sense to recognize the fact that we all live in an abundant universe. Our individual higher source provides more than enough for each and every one of us. Why not work to take everyone to the top? Human nature will dictate that not everyone will achieve the pinnacle. Isn't it at least worth the effort to raise the overall standard?

An amazing thing happens when you invest in others. You tend to get this warm, fuzzy feeling deep in your gut and more importantly, your heart. It just plain feels good! If you're not willing to do it for others because of how they will feel, do it for yourself. You'll feel great and the byproduct will be a whole bunch of people benefiting in some way, shape, or form. As a friend of mine calls it, a happy accident!

VALUE

The "V" in LIVE stands for value. This is a big one in so many ways. Personally, as a Christian, I believe in the Living God and His Son, my Lord and Savior, Jesus Christ. You may believe in Allah, Buddha, Hinduism, the Universe or some other higher source. Belief in a higher source and having faith in something bigger than ourselves is the place where we truly develop an understanding of value. If there is no higher source in your life, you become the top of the pecking order, *numero uno*, the big cheese, and the top dog. But it doesn't make sense that any individual on earth today would hold that position. Rather, we are here to lift each other up and live incredible lives.

We need to value the talents, capabilities, and gifts God or your higher source has given us. We need to be truly grateful for everything in our lives. Sure, that's tough sometimes, but it's worth it in the long haul.

Think about it, there is no reason to grant you any extended blessings if you are not grateful for and appreciative of what you already have. Practice an abundance of appreciation and the attitude of gratitude.

The abundance of appreciation is easy. Thank everyone you see for their contribution in the day you are living. Truly appreciate the various things that people do to make your life better, no matter what it is. Framed properly within your mind, everything and everyone has the potential to benefit another.

Through this journey, I shared five questions that I ask myself as I look back on any situation. 1) What is the lesson in this? 2) What is the gift I have received because of this situation? 3) What did I do to create this in my life? 4) How can it be modified to make it more positive in the future? 5) How is what I've learned going to serve me the rest of my life? By asking these five questions, you develop a desire to make stuff happen, because there is ultimately a positive payoff for you.

Not only does that allow you to appreciate what has happened, it also puts you into a place of gratitude, which is the natural next step. Have an attitude of gratitude. Be truly grateful for everything that happens to you and everything you have in your life.

A funny thing as I type this is, the MercyMe song, "So Long Self", is playing through my iPod. This song talks about *repositioning* yourself from being self-oriented to others-oriented and becoming selfless in our service to others. There are no accidents. This is really what valuing our individual lives becomes all about.

ENJOY

And the "E" in LIVE stands for enjoy. We have all been put on earth to enjoy life to its fullest. There is no grand master plan to make life a miserable, hard, or unpleasant thing. Sure, stuff happens. Stuff will always happen. It's not about the stuff, it's about what we do with it all.

Many times, it has been said that life is not a destination, but a journey. How true! The most interesting thing about that is we are all in control of how we view it. It is within our individual mindsets. We are the most unique beings on earth. We have been granted so many gifts that allow us to experience our surroundings in so many wondrous and mysterious ways.

We have five senses that allow us to take in everything through sight, sound, touch, smell, and taste. These senses allow us to enjoy the beauty of a sunrise, the sound of children laughing, and the hugs of a loved one.

Enjoying life is the reward that is wrapped around everything we do. What you will really achieve is the capacity to live more fully in all aspects of your life. Your mind, your body, and your spirit will hit new heights which will become the new benchmarks for your future.

My wish for you is for you to achieve whatever it is you want to achieve in your life. You are absolutely amazing as you are today. The exciting thought is that where you are is only the beginning of where you are going to go. Imagine the levels you will achieve, the inspiration you will become, and the number of people you will positively impact along the way.

No matter if your desire is to live your legacy fully, or simply understand this information better to help someone you care about, congratulations on your journey!

Nothing in Life is Wasted!

Bad things happen to good people. The main difference is good people overcome bad things!

The events in your life, good or bad, are there to serve you, so you can serve yourself and others. Adopt the mindset that events are not happening *to* you rather they are happening *for* you.

Many times people ask, what types of material they should read or listen to consistently. A couple of things pop into my mind. Many have heard the old axiom, *garbage in, garbage out*! Well, it's really not true. It is far truer to say, *garbage in, garbage stays*! Protecting what you put into your mind is extremely important.

Zig Ziglar put it this way, "You are who you are, and what you are because of what has gone into your mind. You can change who you are and what you are by changing what goes into your mind." Norman Vincent Peale agreed by saying, "Change your thoughts and you change your world."

Personally, the best guidance I can give to answer the question of what to read and what to listen to was written long ago. Philippians 4:8 says:

> *"Whatever is true, whatever is noble, whatever is right, whatever is pure, whatever is lovely, whatever is admirable—if anything is excellent or praiseworthy—think about such things."*

Growing up, our first life course starts with Foundational Knowledge 101 and then progresses up the scale of complexity and difficulty. In reality, so do the lessons in life until we have a Ph.D. in living. Your experiences have already happened, and you cannot change or modify them. But you can take the lessons and solutions learned through everything you have experienced, and make the rest of your life the best of your life!

Thank you for the honor of sharing this with you. Please let me know how I can be of service to you going forward, and how I can assist in your progress. Many will be Blessed by your Inspiration and Legacy!

> *Ultimately, your Legacy is not only what you leave "to" others…*
> *Your Legacy is what you leave "in" others!*

To your continued success!

Scott